THE BELIEVERS' GUIDE TO
MIRACLES
HEALING
IMPARTATION
&ACTIVATION

THE BELIEVERS' GUIDE TO

MIRACLES HEALING IMPARTATION &ACTIVATION

JEFF JANSEN

Published and distributed by Global Fire Publishing –

Cover design: Steve Fryer
Page design: Mark Buschgens

For additional copies of this book and other resources by Jeff Jansen, contact Global Fire Publishing by phone: 1 (615) 867-1124 or by email: info@globalfirepublishing.com

Printed and Manufactured in the United States

ISBN: 978-0-9851128-1-3

CONTENTS

LESSON 6
THE WORKING OF FAITH AND AN ATMOSPHERE FOR MIRACLES

LESSON 7
CREATIVE MIRACLES

LESSON 8
WHY MIRACLES DON'T HAPPEN

LESSON 9
TOTAL FREEDOM FROM THE ROOTS OF SICKNESS AND DISEASE

LESSON 10
MAINTAINING YOUR HEALING

LESSON ONE
my personal journey & your call into the healing ministry

LESSON OBJECTIVES

☞ Describe how hunger, passion, and desire activate God's healing power

☞ Explain why you're called to the healing ministry

☞ Identifying Kingdom keys for jumpstarting God's healing power in your life

During His earthly ministry, Jesus healed countless people from all types of sickness and disease, cast out demons, and performed great signs, wonders, and miracles. However, He never did these incredible acts as God but as a man in right relationship with God. Jesus is our example: His lifestyle is a model that all believers are called to follow—especially concerning the ministry of healing. All believers can lay hands on the sick and see them healed! Jesus sent out the 12 to heal the sick, then the 70, and now, He's sending you! It's time to respond to the call of God on your life and release the miracle power that resides within your spirit man. In this lesson you will: learn how hunger, passion, and desire activate God's healing power; discover that you're actually called to the healing ministry; and learn five keys that will jumpstart God's healing power in your life. Just as the Father sent Jesus into the earth, Jesus is now sending you!

KEY SCRIPTURE PASSAGES

Truly, truly, I say to you, he who believes in Me, the works that I do, he will do also; and greater works than these he will do; because I go to the Father (John 14:12).

And these attesting signs will accompany those who believe: in My name they will drive out demons; they will speak in new languages; They will pick up serpents; and [even] if they drink anything deadly, it will not hurt them; they will lay their hands on the sick, and they will get well (Mark 16:17-18, AMP).

So Jesus said to them again, "Peace be with you; as the Father has sent Me, I also send you" (John 20:21).

I. MY PERSONAL JOURNEY INTO THE MIRACULOUS

Growing up in the small Catholic town of Little Chute, Wisconsin, we didn't see much of anything in relation to revival or miracle ministry. I remember having a strong sense that God was always watching over me, and I was sure that the priest would stand up on Sunday morning to tell everyone my sins. After all, he was God's close friend, so naturally God would tell him everything I was doing wrong. Even as a child I knew that God spoke with us—

even though it was not communicated to me that He did. I remember times as a young boy looking up into the sky and hearing the Lord tell me that I was special to Him. I knew somehow I was different and that one day I would serve the Lord in a full time capacity. One day, the priest asked me at the end of a service what I wanted to be when I grew up. In front of my parents, I told him that I wanted to be a priest and serve the Lord like he did. My parents thought that was funny, and everyone had a great laugh.

As I grew into my teen years I drifted away into experimenting with drugs and alcohol, like so many others. Most of my teen years were a blur as I tried most everything available. I remember stumbling home from parties at night in the dead of winter stoned out of my mind, and instantly, I would become sober as the Lord would walk alongside me and tell me, "It doesn't matter what you do Jeff. I will always love you." I remember falling to my knees and weeping uncontrollably as I felt the love of the Father upon me. Finally, I came to know the Lord at a Spirit-filled Catholic youth group during the Charismatic Renewal. I got saved and filled with the Holy Ghost by tongue-talking, prophesying, Spirit-filled Catholics. I was working with a team that ministered on the streets of Appleton, Wisconsin— sharing our testimonies and leading people to the Lord. Back then things were new and full of adventure. After I graduated from High School, I attended a three-month discipleship training school in Oklahoma City called Agape Force. There, I was introduced to ministries like John Dawson, Winki Pratney, David Wilkerson, Keith Green, Second Chapter of Acts, and many more. I grew quickly during those three months, as did my hunger for God.

John Wimber & Lonnie Frisbee

Shortly thereafter, the ministry I was with wanted to start a Teen Challenge in Appleton. I was asked to go to New York City to evaluate the program and to meet with Don Wilkerson and the leaders there. Little did I know I was about to have an encounter with God that would change my life. While at Teen Challenge in New York, a group of ministers showed up at the door upon their arrival from South Africa. With them were about thirty newly converted young people from California. John Wimber and Lonnie Frisbee had taken a group of new converts with them to South Africa to do healing crusades, and now they were back, sharing the testimonies of all they had encountered there. I was dumb founded as I listened to them speak about blind eyes that were healed and deaf ears that were opened. I read about these things in the Scriptures but was told that God didn't move this way anymore. Lonnie introduced himself to me immediately and said, "You're with me for the rest of the week." Lonnie took me along with him everywhere he went: getting coffee in the inner city, riding through Manhattan and Brooklyn. He talked to me about what God was doing with this generation and about the revival that is upon us.

John and Lonnie decided to put together a last-minute set of meetings in Brooklyn. Lonnie informed me that I would be leading worship with the white-haired guy, John. I had no idea who this guy was as we sang "In His Time" and other classic John Wimber Vineyard songs. For three nights, John and I led worship and Lonnie preached. On the last night, as we were ending in worship, Lonnie took the stage, turned to me in front of the 500, and shouted, "Jeff come here!" I thought that was a little strange, but I took off my guitar, set it down, and walked over to Lonnie on stage. Lonnie stared me down all the way over to him. Then he said, "Lift your hands in the air," so I did. But when I lifted my hands over the top of my head, something happened to me that still sends a chill up my spine. It felt like I took hold of a live 220-amp wire. I shook violently as Lonnie began to call out my healing gift and ministry to the nations. This took place for what seemed like hours. I found myself shaking violently on the ground with people breaking things off of me and ministering to me by the Holy Ghost. It seemed they were speaking the very thoughts going through my mind. The moment I thought something, they spoke it out loud, binding and loosing accordingly.

This was my introduction to the electric power of God. Throughout the course of that week I saw astounding miracles take place. Demons came out shrieking as people were delivered and set free. I had always wondered why the miracles I read about in Scripture didn't happen in our day, but now I was seeing it first hand. I was ruined for God in a new way. I knew that this was what I wanted to do for the rest of my life. I started a new journey into the ministry of the miraculous.

Little did I know not everyone shared the same enthusiasm I did about the ministry of healing. Most rejected my newfound reality of power ministry—I think mostly because of misunderstanding and abuses of past gifting. My sharing of the reality of the Supernatural was met with speculation and harsh resistance. Immediately after Lonnie prayed for me I was praying power prayers over others, prophesying accurately, and people were being healed. I just started doing what I saw them do, and it was working. But as quickly as I got started I met with resistance from my church leaders. They told me I was out of order and was to stop what I was doing. It didn't matter how much I told them of my experience—they didn't want to hear it. I remember crying out to God for an answer, but there was no remedy. Within a short period of time I was completely shut down and non-functioning.

Activated Again

Many things had happened between 1982 and the time I moved with my family to Nashville, Tennessee in 1990. I altogether forgot the miracle ministry as I was completely engulfed in the music industry, writing for Sparrow, Benson Records, Meadowgreen, Tree, and other popular music labels at that time. In 1994 I made a connection with Kelly Willard who did a few projects with Keith Green in the Seventies. She and her husband invited me to a series of meetings with a prophet who was ministering in downtown Nashville. My wife, Jan, and I agreed to go. This turned out to be another pivotal moment for me. The meeting was packed. I saw many of my friends there, as well as many country stars, some of whom I knew personally. The worship ended, and then the ministry began. This prophet ministered powerfully to a few people, calling them out and standing them up to prophesy over them. He called out names and details that seemed to hit home to them. After finishing with just a few people, he moved past me and then asked me my name. The prophet called out my profession, and the people Jan and I were around by name. Then, it happened: he began to prophesy my fivefold miracle ministry into the nations and that God was calling me up and out in this season. This prophet spoke the same word over me that Lonnie Frisbee did twelve years prior. I was in shock. My body was on fire again, and everything turned on again. Immediately, I began to prophesy and see miracles again. It was amazing! Shortly after this, Jan and I were introduced to Bob Jones.

Finding Bob Jones

I asked the Lord for an impartation from Bob. I recall telling the Lord, "Lord, I want Bob Jones." I knew there was much I could learn and receive from Bob as a spiritual father. Within a month, we received an out-of-the-blue invitation from dear friends of ours who met with Bob at his home on a regular basis. It had to be a God-thing, as there was no way we could have orchestrated this meeting on our own. We were excited as we headed out for the 8-9 hour drive down interstate 40.

I remember clearly that we began our journey on the first day of spring. We could never have imagined as we got farther East it would begin to snow. Where we live it rarely snows in the spring. But stranger things have happened, so we marveled at the beauty of the snow as it fell. As nighttime approached, the snow began to accumulate on the side of the road. Then suddenly it began to pile up on the highway. As we approached North Carolina in the Smokey Mountains, we thought we could make it to our destination within one more hour of driving, but traffic suddenly came to a standstill. Cars slipped and slid onto the median and onto the shoulder. There were clearly several inches of snow on the road.

We must have sat in the car for at least an hour before realizing a serious car accident or calamity had completely locked up traffic on Interstate 40 East. No one was going anywhere! We were not close enough to an exit to get off, and the snow continued to pile up! We sympathised with for those who were stuck and had no food in the car. We also quickly realized there were NO public bathrooms on the side of the interstate. When all was said and done, we sat at a complete standstill on the interstate for exactly 8 hours, and it was almost 4:00 a.m. before things began to move again. We found out that a tractor-trailer truck had jack-knifed and blocked the entire highway. The highway opened up as quickly as it locked up, and we were back in motion. We arrived at our friends' house in the wee hours of the morning and were able to catch an hour or so of sleep before the 3-hour drive to Bob's house. The snow had all melted by noon that day!

Amazing confirmation of the purpose of our journey awaited us as we arrived at Bob's house and were introduced to him and his wife. When we first walked into the house, Bob was talking to a group of perhaps 20 people about his first meeting with Mike Bickle when he was in Kansas City. Apparently, there were people who didn't know Bob and questioned who Bob Jones really was. Some wondered if he was a "true prophet." Bob recalled how he told Mike Bickle, "Well, you will know who the true prophets are when it snows on the first day of Spring, and as quickly as it comes, it all melts and goes away by noon."

Mike Bickle said, "Now I know this Bob Jones is a false prophet" (because the weather had been unseasonably warm that year and the possibility of snow was very remote). But it happened exactly like Bob Jones said that year, and Mike Bickle and others were amazed!

So it happened with us exactly as it happened with Bob on the first day of spring—Bob looked over at us and winked.

That day Bob prayed for us and took us "up" into Heaven. There was no natural source for wind inside his home, but we felt the strong wind of the Heaven blowing all around us. "Ya feel that? Feel the wind whipping up on you!" Bob said.

Since our meeting with Bob Jones in 2002, we are on a fast track into the Glory of God. I could go on to tell you of angelic encounters that have brought amazing dimensions of Kingdom manifestation into my life. As of today, we have ministered in more than 65 nations in crusades, conferences, and Glory Explosion meetings. We have seen tens of thousands healed, saved, and delivered, and we have just begun. My prayer is that as you read this book and study its contents, you would receive an impartation of healing, signs, and wonders that would launch you into the ministry of miracles.

God Bless You
Jeff Jansen

II. YOUR CALL INTO THE HEALING MINISTRY

A. *Believers* will do greater things than Jesus did—that's what He said! (John 14:12).

B. Signs follow those who *believe*—like speaking in tongues, casting out demons, and healing the sick (Mark 16:17-18).

C. The prayer of *faith* heals the sick, not just the prayer of the great healing evangelist of our day (James 5:15).

D. Just as Jesus was sent into the world to bring healing and release the power of God, you are sent too! (John 20:21).

III. FIVE KEYS TO RELEASING GOD'S HEALING POWER IN YOUR LIFE

Listed below are five keys that you can use to help jumpstart the power of God in your life. Because I go into greater detail in the following lessons on unlocking the supernatural realm and the healing and miracle ministry, I'm only giving you a few very practical keys to begin . These keys are foundational for anybody who wants to move in the healing ministry.

KEY 1: Relationship with the Holy Spirit

A. Fellowship with the Holy Spirit (2 Cor. 13:14).

B. This whole thing we call "Christianity" is actually about intimate relationship with God. It's not a set a rules we are forced to obey, but a Person we choose to follow, to love, and to waste our entire lives on. There is nothing in this life, or the next for that matter, that can be compared to the surpassing value of knowing Jesus Christ—everything else is rubbish (Phil. 3:8). The momentary afflictions we experience in this life are minor in comparison to the exquisite glory that will be "...*revealed to us and in us and for us and conferred on us*" (Rom. 8:18, AMP)! First and foremost, we are called to love God with all of our heart, soul, mind, and strength (Mark 12:30). At the end of the day this is what matters most. Ask yourself, "Am I living for myself or for God? Am I living to please man so I can gain acceptance and approval, or am I staying true to the word of the Lord over my life?"

KEY 2: A Passionate Thirst and Desperation for His Presence and Power

The Lord pours out His Spirit on dry and thirsty ground. If you want to experience the power of God and the anointing of the Holy Spirit, passionate desperation is often a prerequisite for receiving a touch from above.

A. God pours out water (His Spirit) on dry and thirsty ground (Isa. 44:3).

B. God draws near to you when you draw near

to Him (James 4:8).

C. Ask, seek, and knock (Matt. 7:7-8).

D. God gives good gifts—Ask for the Holy Spirit (Luke 11:13).

KEY 3: Meditate on the Scriptures

A. Read the Gospels and watch how Jesus preached the Kingdom Gospel, healed the sick, delivered the oppressed, and performed miracles, signs, and wonders.

B. Read the book of Acts and watch as the early church exploded when the Holy Spirit was poured out.

C. Study the Word—rightly divide the Word of Truth (2 Tim. 2:15).

KEY 4: Cultivating a Heart of Faith and Belief

A. God is pleased when you have faith (Heb. 11:6).

B. True faith is a matter of the heart, not of the mind (Rom. 10:10).

C. From faith to faith to faith (Rom. 1:17).

D. Cultivate Faithfulness (Ps. 37:3).

E. Hearing with Faith (Gal. 3:2).

F. All things are possible to him who believes (Mark 9:23).

KEY 5: Total Surrender and Quick Obedience

Total surrender is one of the most important steps for catapulting you into deeper realms of the Spirit. It is, unfortunately, one of the places most people get hung up. Living in compromise and following the Holy Spirit half-heartedly is like trying to swim across the Atlantic with a millstone strapped to your neck—It's impossible! You can't go where the Holy Spirit wants to lead you if you're not willing to deny yourself and take up your cross. It's decision-making time: when He says, "Go!" will you go? When He says "No," will you lay it down? Let me tell you, if you choose to follow the Holy Spirit with all your heart and come to Him with open hands, not holding on to anything in this life, but living in complete and total surrender, you won't be sorry—you won't regret it. There is a greater glory waiting for those who choose to follow Him... a far greater glory.

A. Following Jesus means denying yourself—losing yourself—in order to find yourself (Matt. 16:24-25)

B. Full submission to God is the key for being empowered to overcome the enemy (James 4:7-8).

C. Obedience to God prepares a place in us for Him to rest (John 14:23).

D. Loving God means we obey Him (1 John 5:3).

REFLECTION QUESTIONS

1. Why does hunger activate God's healing power?

    _____

    _____

2. What are some things that get you excited about healing?

    _____

    _____

3. Do you believe you are called to the healing ministry?

    _____

    _____

4. Who will do greater works than Jesus?

    _____

    _____

5. Who will lay their hands on the sick and see them recover?

    _____

    _____

6. What type of prayer heals the sick?

    _____

    _____

7. Out of the five keys listed for jumpstarting God's healing power in your life, which ones are you *currently practicing* and feel you are *strong in?* (It could be all or none.)

    _____

    _____

8. Out of the five keys listed for jumpstarting God's healing power in your life, which ones are you *not currently practicing* or you feel you *need improvement in?* (It could be all or none.)

    _____

    _____

Life Application

Grab your journal or notebook and get alone with God. Press into God with a Holy desperation asking Him for the nations as your inheritance. Ask for His healing power to flow through you and for opportunity and boldness to pray for the sick and the afflicted. Ask the Holy Spirit to show you how He wants to use you in the healing ministry to be His hands and feet in the earth. Journal anything He shows you and any encounters you have.

Prayer

Take a few minutes to write, in the lines provided below, a sincere prayer from your heart asking for God to use you in the healing ministry. Use this also as an opportunity to get right with God and confess concealed sin or disobedience. If there is anyone that you have unforgiveness towards, forgive them completely and release them to God. Ask God to forgive you for holding unforgiveness in your heart and to remove all roots of bitterness. Ask the Father to apply the shed blood of Jesus Christ over your mind, soul, spirit, body, and entire being. Allow the Holy Spirit to fill you anew.

LESSON TWO

the kingdom mandate

LESSON OBJECTIVES

☞ Examine the Gospel of the Kingdom

☞ Inspect what the Kingdom actually is

☞ Discover why Miracles and Healings follow the Gospel of the Kingdom

☞ Learn about the Person of the Holy Spirit

☞ Examine the dynamics of growing in relationship with Him

☞ Discover why the Holy Spirit releases the Kingdom of God

In this lesson we will discuss the Gospel of the Kingdom. This is the Gospel Jesus preached, the Gospel His disciples preached, and the Gospel we are called to preach, demonstrate, and manifest in the earth. We have received given a *Kingdom Mandate* directly from the throne of God to walk as kings and priests in the earth and to bring restoration to creation through the power of Kingdom decrees. Because the Spirit of the living Christ resides in us, we are the expression of God in the earth—we are carriers and dispensers of God's Kingdom, power, and glory. In this lesson, you will also learn about the Person of the Holy Spirit—who He is and what He does. We will discuss how the Holy Spirit operates in our lives and ministries and gives us access to walking in the supernatural. Get ready to be empowered by the Holy Spirit to release the Kingdom of God already dwelling within you!

KEY SCRIPTURE PASSAGES

"My kingdom is not of this world...." Therefore Pilate said to Him, "So You are a king?" Jesus answered, "You say correctly that I am a king. For this I have been born, and for this I have come into the world..." (John 18:36-37).

Jesus summoned His twelve disciples and gave them authority over unclean spirits, to cast them out, and to heal every kind of disease and every kind of sickness. "And as you go, preach, saying, 'The kingdom of heaven is at hand.' Heal the sick, raise the dead, cleanse the lepers, cast out demons. Freely you received, freely give" (Matt. 10:1, 7-8).

Pray, then, in this way: "Your kingdom come. Your will be done, on earth as it is in heaven" (Matt. 6:9-10).

But you shall receive power (ability, efficiency, and might) when the Holy Spirit has come upon you, and you shall be My witnesses in Jerusalem and all Judea and Samaria and to the ends (the very bounds) of the earth (Acts 1:8, AMP).

Pray, then, in this way: "Your kingdom come. Your will be done, on earth as it is in heaven" (Matt. 6:9-10).

I. ON EARTH AS IT IS IN HEAVEN

The physical realm of earth was created to be an extension of God's Kingdom dominion that exists in heaven. The physical realm was patterned after the supernatural realm. Before the natural realm existed, there were only heavenly (supernatural) realms with heavenly (supernatural) beings. God ruled this supernatural realm from His throne, the heart of heaven, and angels executed His every word.

The Garden of Eden was designed to be heaven on earth—the supernatural realm of heaven expressed in the realm of the natural. However, as we know, when the fall of man occurred, we cut ourselves off from communion with God and legal access to the supernatural realm. But, through the shed blood of Jesus, we have an open door to commune with God and can access the supernatural realm of heaven at any time (Heb. 4:16, 10:19-22, 12:22-24).

When Jesus taught His disciples to pray, He said to pray to the Father who is in heaven and to pray this way: "*Your kingdom come. Your will be done, on earth as it is in heaven*" (Matt. 6:10). Many people wonder what God's will is. In the verse above, we are shown that His *will* is *His Kingdom being manifested in the earth*. Where does His Kingdom exist now? In heaven. Where does He want to extend His Kingdom now? On earth.

_____

_____

_____

_____

_____

_____

_____

_____

_____

_____

_____

_____

_____

_____

_____

_____

_____

_____

II. IT'S A GOVERNMENTAL KINGDOM — NOT RELIGION

The word *kingdom* can be broken into two parts: "king's domain," or the "dominion of the king." When referring to God's Kingdom, we are talking about everything that has been subdued and is under the rule and dominion of King Jesus.

In the Bible, the *Kingdom of heaven* and the *Kingdom of God* are used synonymously. They both refer to the dominion of God, which first exists in the eternal realm of heaven from the throne of God and then extends into the physical realm of earth.

When Jesus came in the flesh, He didn't come to start a religion. He didn't even come to start a church. He came to establish His Father's Kingdom—which already existed in heaven—on Earth. He came to the Earth as Heaven's beachhead in order to reclaim all that was lost & stolen during the fall (Gen. 3). When Jesus hung from the cross and shouted, "It is finished!" He was declaring the end of an Old Covenant and the beginning of a New Covenant. In that speck of sand on the seashore of time, He defeated every power in hell and every principality in the heavens. He opened up and became a New and Living Way, giving us unlimited access to His presence and grace in His Kingdom (Heb. 10:19-22; John 14:6; Heb. 4:16).

When Jesus came in the flesh, it was only the beginning of His Kingdom being established on the earth. From that point in time, His Kingdom has continually grown and advanced, taking authority and bringing all things under His rule and dominion. There are many areas that have yet to be brought into submission to His Kingdom—many areas where the Kingdom of God must be extended in love and power. We know, though, that the Kingdom of God will continually advance in the earth until the day He returns in glory for His spotless bride. In that time, the fullness of His Kingdom will be manifested and every knee will bow and every tongue confess that Jesus is Lord (Rev. 2:10-11).

A. Kingdom Defined

  1. *Kingdom* (Merriam-Webster Dictionary)

   a) *archaic*: Kingship

   b) a politically organized community or major territorial unit having a monarchical form of government headed by a king or queen

   c) the eternal kingship of God: the realm in which God's will is fulfilled

   d) a realm or region in which something is dominant; an area or sphere in which one holds a preeminent position

  2. King's Dominion: The Dominion of the King

   a) *King* (Merriam-Webster Dictionary)

    i) a male monarch of a major territorial unit; *especially*: one whose position is hereditary and who rules for

_____

_____

_____

_____

_____

_____

_____

_____

_____

_____

_____

_____

_____

_____

_____

_____

_____

_____

_____

_____

life; a paramount chief

ii). God, Christ

iii) one that holds a preeminent position; *especially*: a chief among competitors

b) *Dominion* (Merriam-Webster Dictionary)

i) domain

ii) supreme authority: sovereignty

iii) absolute ownership

3. What parts make up a Kingdom?

a) A Kingdom has a *King* [Jesus].

b) A Kingdom has *territory, land, property,* etc. [heaven being extended on earth].

c) A Kingdom has *citizens* [not religious members, but citizens who have rights; believers].

d) A Kingdom has a constitution [the Word of God].

e) A Kingdom has laws [walking in love (John 13:34), walking in the Spirit (Gal. 5:14-25)].

f) A Kingdom has a government and ruling authorities [sons and daughters of God].

g) A Kingdom has a code of ethics and beliefs [statements of faith that are revealed in the Word of God].

                             _____

h) A Kingdom has privileges [citizens of a Kingdom have special privileges foreigners don't have].

i) A Kingdom has an army, military forces, etc. [angelic hosts, beings, warriors, etc.].

B. Kingdom Characteristics

   1. The Kingdom was Prepared for You in Eternity.

      a) Matt. 25:34

      b) Eph. 3:11

      c) 1 Peter 1:19-20

   2. The Kingdom of God is Everlasting.

      a) Ps. 145:13

      b) Dan. 7:13-14

   3. The Kingdom of God is Ever-Expanding and Ever-Growing.

      a) Isa. 9:6-7

      b) Matt. 13:31

      c) 1 Cor. 15:24-25

      d) Hag. 2:9

4. The Kingdom of God is Dominant over all Other Kingdoms.

    a) Dan. 2:44

    b) 1 Cor. 15:24-27

    c) Rev. 11:15

III. THE GOSPEL THAT NEEDS TO BE PREACHED!

Kingdom attributes and truths have been preached throughout history, many successfully manifesting powerful Kingdom realities. Each of these truths is essential for establishing the Kingdom on the earth. Even today, there are many truths being preached: salvation, deliverance, healing, miracles, etc. These are wonderful within themselves, but *they alone* are not the Gospel of the Kingdom—they accompany the preaching of the Gospel of the Kingdom. It's important for us to understand that Jesus did not come preaching salvation. He didn't preach miracles, nor did He preach deliverance or healing. Jesus came preaching the Gospel of the Kingdom.

> *But He said to them, "I must preach the good news (the Gospel) of the kingdom of God to the other cities [and towns] also, for I was sent for this [purpose]"* (Luke 4:43, AMP).

This is a powerful statement. Jesus said He was sent to preach the Gospel of the Kingdom: "*... for I was sent for this [purpose]*" (AMP). Jesus brought salvation, healing, and deliverance. He performed miracles, signs, and wonders; however, He did it all while preaching the Gospel of the Kingdom of God.

According to Mark 16:15, we are commissioned to *"Go into all the world and preach the gospel to every creature"* (NKJV). Since we've been given such a great commission, it's essential we receive an understanding of the Gospel we're called to preach. The word *Gospel* means "good news." As followers of Christ we have been given a mandate to preach the good news of His Kingdom. What is the good news? Simply, it's that the Kingdom of heaven has arrived on earth (is at hand) and King Jesus is on the throne (Matt. 10:7-10). And for a little more good news, we are seated with Christ in heaven (Eph. 2:6) and have the privilege and authority to extend His Kingdom on earth as sons and daughters of the Father.

IV. WHO PREACHED THE KINGDOM GOSPEL?

A. Jesus—from Start to Finish

1. At the *beginning* of His ministry:

From that time Jesus began to preach and say, "Repent, for the kingdom of heaven is at hand" (Matt. 4:17).

2. *During* His Ministry, the majority of Jesus' teachings and parables were about the Kingdom of God and the Kingdom of Heaven. (Read Matthew.)

3. Directly *before His crucifixion:*

_____
_____
_____
_____
_____
_____
_____
_____
_____
_____
_____
_____
_____
_____
_____
_____
_____
_____
_____
_____

Jesus answered, "My kingdom is not of this world. If My kingdom were of this world, then My servants would be fighting so that I would not be handed over to the Jews; but as it is, My kingdom is not of this realm" (John 18:36).

4. *After His resurrection and towards the end* of His earthly ministry:

To these He also presented Himself alive after His suffering, by many convincing proofs, appearing to them over a period of forty days and speaking of the things concerning the kingdom of God (Acts 1:3).

B. The Twelve

And He called the twelve together, and gave them power and authority over all the demons and to heal diseases. And He sent them out to proclaim the kingdom of God and to perform healing (Luke 9:1-2).

C. The Seventy

Now after this the Lord appointed seventy others, and sent them in pairs ahead of Him to every city and place where He Himself was going to come "and heal those in it who are sick, and say to them, 'The kingdom of God has come near to you'" (Luke 10:1,9).

D. Paul

1. *And he entered the synagogue and continued speaking out boldly for three months, reasoning and persuading them about the kingdom of God (Acts 19:8).*

2. *When they had set a day for Paul, they came to him at his lodging in large numbers; and he was explaining to them by solemnly testifying about the kingdom of God and trying to persuade them concerning Jesus, from both the Law of Moses and from the Prophets, from morning until evening. And he stayed two full years in his own rented quarters and was welcoming all who came to him, preaching the kingdom of God and teaching concerning the Lord Jesus Christ with all openness, unhindered (Acts 28:23, 30-31).*

E. Others

1. *Now in those days John the Baptist came preaching in the wilderness of Judea, saying, "Repent, for the kingdom of heaven is at hand" (Matt. 3:1-2).*

2. *But when they believed the good news (the Gospel) about the kingdom of God and the name of Jesus Christ (the Messiah) as Philip preached it, they were baptized, both men and women (Acts 8:12, AMP).*

F. The Gospel to the End!

_____
_____
_____
_____
_____
_____
_____
_____
_____
_____
_____
_____
_____
_____
_____
_____
_____
_____

This gospel of the kingdom shall be preached in the whole world as a testimony to all the nations, and then the end will come (Matt. 24:14).

V. MIRACLES AND HEALINGS IN THE KINGDOM OF GOD: A GOSPEL OF POWER

A. The Kingdom of God is a Kingdom of Power (1 Cor. 4:20).

B. Attesting signs follow believers such as healings, new languages, and casting out of demons (Mark 16:17-18).

C. Heal the sick, raise the dead, cleanse the lepers, cast out demons (Matt. 10:7-8).

D. We are called to do greater works than Jesus— He said it! (John 14:12).

E. The power of signs and wonders follow the preaching of the Gospel (Rom. 15:19).

F. The Holy Spirit gives us the power to witness about Jesus and be effective ministers of the Gospel (Acts 1:8).

G. We can pray for signs, wonders, and healings to happen through the name of Jesus, just like the early church (Acts 4:29-31).

VI. THE PERSON OF THE HOLY SPIRIT

The Holy Spirit is a Person we are meant to commune and fellowship with. He is the third Person in the Godhead—completely equal to God the Father and God the Son. The Holy Spirit is God: He is eternal and divine. Some refer to the Spirit of God as an "it" or "itself." Biblically, this is incorrect; the pronouns the Bible always uses to speak of the Holy Spirit are "Him" and "Himself."

In numerous places in Scripture we see the Holy Spirit portraying characteristics of a Person, comparable to God, the Father and God, the Son. He demonstrates that He has intellect, emotions, thoughts, feelings, and a will. He is omnipresent to believers; He knows the depths of God, making Him all knowing. He is the all powerful, omnipotent, eternal Spirit of God, who has no beginning and no end.

There are many reasons why it is important to understand that the Holy Spirit is a Person and that He is also God. In the Old Testament, the people of God could say, "We have God *for* us, and we have God *with* us," but they could never say, "We have God in us." New Testament believers are the tabernacles of the Most High God: He lives in us by His precious Holy Spirit becoming one with our spirit. We not only have God *for* us and *with* us, but *in* us and *one spirit* with us!

If the Holy Spirit were simply a power, force, or influence and was not a Person, we would try to do all we could to get a hold of that power. But because the Holy

Spirit is a Person, we want Him to get a hold of us. If the Holy Spirit were a force, we would use it to accomplish our will and agenda, and we would eventually slip into pride. But because He is a Person we partner with Him to accomplish His will. We are humbled by the thought of God wanting to use us. It's not really a matter of attaining something we don't have, but of surrendering to the Holy Spirit so that His power and anointing can flow through us. From a place of humility and brokenness before the Lord, we come to value His all-sufficient grace that's perfected in our weakness. On many accounts, I've heard that much-repeated Christian phrase, "Faith is spelled R-I-S-K." It's really true. Exercising genuine faith is being positioned in a place of total dependency on our Father in heaven. If you're in a place where you will utterly fail if the Holy Spirit doesn't do something, you're in a really good spot!

The Holy Spirit displays numerous characteristics only a person could have: He displays intellect by searching and examining the deep things of God; He instructs, teaches, and guides; He has a will, displays emotion, and can speak; and, He can be insulted, lied to, blasphemed, resisted, and even grieved.

A. The Holy Spirit Has an Intellect

    1. He searches and knows all things, including the depths of God (1 Cor. 2:10).

    2. He prays, intercedes, searches hearts, has a mind, and knows the will of God (Rom. 8:26-27).

3. He teaches believers all things (John 14:26).   _____

4. He instructs (Neh. 9:20).   _____

5. He testifies (John 15:26).   _____

6. He guides, speaks, hears, and discloses (John 16:12-15).   _____

_____

B. The Holy Spirit Has a Will   _____

   1. He distributes gifts as He wills (1Cor. 12:11).   _____

   2. He appoints and assigns as He wills (Acts 20:28).   _____

_____

C. The Holy Spirit Has Emotions   _____

   1. The Love of the Spirit (Rom. 15:30).   _____

   2. Don't grieve Him (Eph. 4:30).   _____

D. The Holy Spirit Can Speak   _____

   1. He calls out and cries, "Abba, Father!" from our hearts (Gal. 4:6).   _____

   2. He calls, sets apart, and sends out believers for ministry (Acts 13:2,4).   _____

   3. He speaks to the church (Rev. 2:7; Heb. 3:7).   _____

_____

E. Other   _____

   1. He can be grieved (Eph. 4:30).   _____

      a) Remember, this letter is addressed to the church in Ephesus. Paul is not writing to unbelievers but to born again   _____

_____

_____

_____

_____

_____

_____

_____

_____

_____

_____

_____

_____

_____

_____

_____

_____

_____

Christians.

b) In this verse, grieving the Holy Spirit is specifically referring to any type of unwholesome talk (bitterness, clamor, slander, malice, wrath, anger, gossip, etc.). We actually hurt the Holy Spirit by careless speech.

2. He can be insulted (Heb. 10:29).

3. He can be lied to (Acts 5:3-4).

4. He can be blasphemed (Matt. 12:31; Mark 3:29).

5. He can be resisted (Acts 7:51; Zech. 7:11-13).

6. He can be quenched (1 Thess. 5:19).

a) Paul is writing to the church of the Thessalonians; He is instructing born-again believers not to quench the Spirit.

b) Quenching the Spirit is like pouring water on a fire. We can hinder, resist, and quench the Holy Spirit from moving by having doubt and unbelief in our hearts, and by despising prophetic words (see vs. 20).

VII. THE HOLY SPIRIT IS OUR KINGDOM GUIDE

Jesus didn't come to Earth so He could start a religion. He wasn't nailed to the cross so we could do church. Jesus came to establish and advance the multidimensional, supernatural, heavenly Kingdom on the earth.

What is God's will? His Kingdom. What should earth look like? Heaven. How do we know this? Because this is how Jesus taught us to pray: *"Your kingdom come. Your will be done, on earth as it is in heaven"* (Matt. 6:10). Jesus flawlessly modeled what it looks like to manifest the Kingdom of heaven on earth. He demonstrated miracle after miracle; walked in perfect love; overcame temptation; lived righteously, and revealed the Father. How was He able to do this? Was it because He walked as God on earth? Nope.

The Bible says that Jesus emptied Himself, took the form of a bondservant and was made in the likeness of men (Phil. 2:5-8). Jesus never performed a single miracle as God while on the earth as. Every supernatural feat He displayed was as a man in right relationship with God. He showed us what *any Spirit filled man* can *do* and *be* when in right relationship with the Father.

So what was His secret? Why did the power of God flood His ministry? How do we allow the power of God to move through our lives to manifest the Kingdom of heaven on earth? It is only by the Holy Spirit!

REFLECTION QUESTIONS

1. The physical realm of earth was designed to be an extension of what?

    _____

    _____

2. Concerning the Kingdom, how did Jesus teach us to pray?

    _____

    _____

3. What are four characteristics of God's Kingdom?

    _____

    _____

4. What is the Gospel of the Kingdom? What do we preach?

    _____

    _____

5. Who preached the Gospel of the Kingdom?

    _____

    _____

6. What are some scriptures that teach us that the Kingdom of God is a Kingdom of power?

    _____

    _____

7. Who gives us power to be witnesses of Jesus and effective Kingdom ministers?

_____

_____

8. What are some ways you plan on growing in intimacy with the Holy Spirit?

_____

_____

Life Application

This lesson holds foundational principles for understanding the Kingdom mechanics that exist in the rest of this manual. Take time to go back through this lesson with your Bible open, and highlight or underline each Scripture verse referenced (or write it on a separate sheet of paper). Ask the Holy Spirit to open your eyes and give you revelation concerning each passage as you read over it several times. What type of Kingdom ministry do you see yourself operating in? Write down several ways on how to implement genuine Kingdom living in your daily routine. In what ways can you apply these Kingdom principles in your life? Start doing the things you've written as led by the Holy Spirit.

Prayer

Father God, I ask that Your Kingdom would come and Your will would be done in my life as it is done in heaven. Give me eyes to see and ears to hear concerning the mysteries of the Kingdom of heaven. I dedicate myself to seeking first Your Kingdom and Your righteousness—let Your Kingdom of Power and Glory invade my life. Today is a new day—a day of fresh beginnings and of discovery. Lift me from this earthly realm to the place in the heavenlies where I see and perceive the unseen by faith and pull it into the NOW. Use me as a citizen of heaven to advance Your governmental Kingdom in the earth. In Jesus' name, Amen!

LESSON THREE

the redemptive nature of God

LESSON OBJECTIVES

☛ Examine the redemptive nature of God through Calvary

☛ Examine the seven redemptive names of God

When Jesus died on the cross, a veil was torn that gave us complete and total access to the holy of holies—the presence of God—heaven's storehouse. Everything we could ever need or desire comes from our heavenly Father. He is the giver of every good and perfect gift. The blessings of financial provision, healing, deliverance, His near presence, and everlasting peace and joy are all given to us through the shedding of Christ's blood, which is our inheritance as sons and daughters of God. Through examining the seven redemptive names of Jehovah, we can come to a more complete and accurate understanding of the nature of God and our birthright in the Kingdom of God.

KEY SCRIPTURE PASSAGES

Blessed be the God and Father of our Lord Jesus Christ, who has blessed us with every spiritual blessing in the heavenly places in Christ (Eph. 1:3).

And if you belong to Christ [are in Him Who is Abraham's Seed], then you are Abraham's offspring and [spiritual] heirs according to promise (Gal. 3:29, AMP).

...so that He might redeem those who were under the Law, that we might receive the adoption as sons. Because you are sons, God has sent forth the Spirit of His Son into our hearts, crying, "Abba! Father!" Therefore you are no longer a slave, but a son; and if a son, then an heir through God (Gal. 4:5-7).

I. THE HEART OF REDEMPTION: CALVARY

A. Man's need for Redemption—Fallen from Grace

   1. In the Garden of Eden, Adam sinned (disobeyed God) and opened up—not only to mankind, but to the entire created natural realm—the effects of sin: death.

    a) Gen. 3:1-24

    b) Rom. 5:14

    c) 1 Cor. 15:22

2. The Sinfulness of Man

    a) All have sinned and fallen short of living in God's glory. We all need redemption from sin (Rom. 3:23).

    b) The heart of man is deceitful and wicked—our old heart and old nature (Jer. 17:9).

    c) Evil comes from within our old heart and nature. Each person needs a new heart and new nature (Mark 7:20-23).

3. The Law of Sin and Death: The Curse

    a) Spiritual and physical death—cut off from God (Gen. 2:17, 3:1-24).

    b) Sin equals death (Rom. 6:23; James 1:14-15).

    c) Sin and the Law (Rom. 7:5).

    d) Adam didn't just subject mankind to a curse, he opened a door that allowed sin to enter and spread through *the entire created natural realm* (Rom. 8:19-22; Gen. 3:1-24).

_____

_____

_____

_____

_____

_____

_____

_____

_____

_____

_____

_____

_____

_____

_____

_____

_____

_____

B. Five Accomplishments of Calvary

1. Jesus *restored us to right relationship with God the Father.* It gives us the ability to hear His voice, enter His presence, and know Him intimately as Father and Friend.

    a) In Christ, God's love, nature, and name is revealed (John 17:26).

    b) In Christ, we are reconciled to God (2 Cor. 5:18-19).

    c) Eternal life is knowing the Father and Jesus Christ (John 17:3).

    d) We can enter His presence boldly and with confidence (Heb. 4:14-16).

2. Jesus *redeemed us from the curse and from the law of sin and death.* The shed blood of Jesus completely and thoroughly removes our sins and transgressions from us.

    a) Jesus has redeemed us from the curse of the law so that we might receive the promise (Gal. 3:13).

    b) Jesus became sin so we would not only be freed from sin, but also become the righeousness of God (2 Cor. 5:21).

    c) Released from the Law (Rom. 7:6)

3. Jesus has *opened a way for us to receive a new heart and a new nature.* We become new creations in Christ Jesus!

    a) We become new creations in Christ (2 Cor. 5:17).

    b) Put on the new man, the new self, and the new nature (Eph. 4:24).

    c) Taking out the heart of stone [law] and putting in a heart of flesh [a heart that is alive and pliable] (Ezek. 36:26)

4. Jesus *supplied a way for us to be adopted into the Family of God.* He became our older brother, and His Father became our Father.

    a) Adopted as sons (Gal. 4:5-7)

    b) Spirit of Adoption (Rom. 8:15)

    c) Predestined for Adoption (Eph. 1:4-5)

    d) Jesus calls us brothers [brethren]— bringing many sons to glory (Heb. 2:10-18).

5. Jesus brought us into the Kingdom of heaven and seated us with Him at the right hand of God, giving us *access to our eternal inheritance now.* Because we are family, we have an inheritance, and because we are in Christ, we receive the promise and blessings of Abraham.

_____
_____
_____
_____
_____
_____
_____
_____
_____
_____
_____
_____
_____
_____
_____
_____
_____
_____
_____
_____

a) Seated in the heavenlies *with* Christ and *in* Christ (Eph. 2:6; Col. 3:1-3)

b) We are children of God and heirs with Christ (Rom. 8:15-17).

c) Sons are heirs (Gal. 4:5-7).

d) We have an eternal inheritance (Gal. 4:5-7).

II. THE SEVEN REDEMPTIVE NAMES OF JEHOVAH

Listed below you'll find the seven redemptive names of Jehovah. Each redemptive name points to Calvary, the pinnacle of redemption for mankind. The shedding of Christ's blood has echoed through eternity: it is the majesty of our Father's immense love for the world. Jesus, as Redeemer, has violently ripped the veil that for so long kept mankind from tasting the precious presence of Eternal God. Every principality and power was and is made a public spectacle by the cross. Every barrier holding us back from His glory has been trampled underfoot. Now, by His shed blood, we have access to the Holy of Holies—to boldly and, with confidence, come before the throne of grace—to taste of His eternal power, of the age to come, and to partake of His Divine Nature. The storerooms of heaven are open. Let's study the names of Jehovah to gain a greater understanding of the inheritance we possess in Christ.

» Although the New Testament Scripture passages listed below do not contain the Hebrew words we are examining, they do portray the specific aspect of God's nature that we're studying.

» Next to each Jehovah Name, please fill in the blank (e.g. The Lord *my Shepherd*, The Lord *our Banner*, etc.).

A. Jehovah Rapha: The Lord _____.

    1. Ex. 15:26

    2. Isa. 53:5

    3. 1 Peter 2:24

B. Jehovah-Jireh: The Lord _____.

    1. Gen. 22:8-14

    2. Phil. 4:19

C. Jehovah-Shalom: The Lord _____.

    1. Judges 6:24

    2. Isa. 9:6

    3. Isa. 53:5

    4. Eph. 2:14

    5. Rom. 5:1

D. Jehovah-Nissi: The Lord _____.

    1. Ex. 17:15

_____

_____

_____

_____

_____

_____

_____

_____

_____

_____

_____

_____

_____

_____

_____

_____

_____

_____

_____

_____

2. Isa. 49:22, AMP

E. Jehovah-Rohi: The Lord _____.

    1. Ps. 23:1

    2. John 10:11

F. Jehovah-Tsidkenu: The Lord _____.

    1. Jer. 23:6

    2. 1 Cor. 1:30

G. Jehovah-Shammah: The Lord _____.

    1. Ez. 48:35

    2. Matt. 18:20

    3. Ps. 139:7-8

    4. Eph. 4:9-10

III. TOTAL SALVATION: SPIRIT, SOUL, AND BODY

One of the reasons we don't see people healed when we pray for them is because there is still a part of us that says, "Lord, if it's Your will…" or "Father, if it's Your timing…." Deep down inside, these thoughts and feelings are actually doubts about whether or not God is really *willing* to heal them. "We know He can," we say, but will

He? YES! It is absolutely God's will to heal! When we understand this, and when we really get it, we can pray with expectation—real faith that the Spirit of God is going to touch the person! Not only *can* God heal; He *will* heal! There's a difference.

A. *"I am willing; be cleansed."* Not only can God heal you; He will heal you (Luke 5:12-13).

B. Jesus healed everyone (Matt. 4:24; 8:16; Luke 6:17-19).

C. We are called to do the same works as Jesus, and even greater (John 14:12).

D. The disciples' commission (Matt. 10:1,7-8; Luke 10:1-11)

E. Divine health/healing is a process; it takes time (Luke 17:12-14).

F. Miracles are instant (John 5:1-9).

G. Warring against Sickness

H. Jehovah-Rapha, the God who heals (Ex. 15:26).

I. Out of Egypt… silver, gold, and no one feeble (Ps. 105:37)

J. Types and shadows of Calvary (Ex. 15:22-25; Num. 21:4-9)

K. By His stripes… (Isa. 53:1-5)

L. Forgiveness and healing go together (Isa. 33:24; Mark 2:3-12).

M. Sozo: Complete and Total Salvation

_____

_____

_____

_____

_____

_____

_____

_____

1. Sozo defined: Saved, Healed, and Delivered—Spirit, Soul, and Body.

2. Sozo prophesied (Joel 2:31; Acts 2:21).

3. Sozo is salvation for the spirit (Matt. 1:21; Rom. 10:13).

4. Sozo is deliverance for the soul (Luke 8:36).

5. Sozo is healing for the body (Mark 5:34; James 5:15).

REFLECTION QUESTIONS

1. Why did mankind need redemption?

    _____

    _____

2. Where have we all fallen from?

    _____

    _____

3. What are a few things that Calvary accomplished?

    _____

    _____

4. Please explain below what it means to be a new creation in Christ:

_____

_____

5. We are heirs with Christ. What does this mean?

_____

_____

6. What are the seven Hebrew names of Jehovah and what do they mean?

_____

_____

7. How do we know it's God's will to heal us?

_____

_____

8. What does the Greek word Sozo mean? How does this affect you personally?

_____

_____

Life Application

Grab your journal or notebook and get alone with God. Go back through this lesson to examine the seven names of Jehovah and the scripture passages referenced. Ask the Lord to reveal to you His character and nature. Ask Him to show you why Calvary is the heart of redemption, and why you possess an eternal inheritance as a child of God. Ask Him to show you the inheritance He has freely given you to walk in now—the inheritance you possess. Write down what He shows you, and ask Him to launch you into walking in the fullness of your inheritance.

Prayer

Father God, thank you for reconciling me to Yourself through your son Jesus Christ. It's my aim and greatest endeavor to know you as intimately as You can be known. I ask that you would reveal to me the inheritance I possess as a blood-bought, Spirit-filled, overcoming child of the Most High God! Reveal to me Your character as revealed in the seven names we studied in this lesson, in Jesus' name, Amen!

LESSON FOUR

the assurance of covenant healing

LESSON OBJECTIVES

- ☛ Examine our covenant with God and the power of covenant for the believer
- ☛ Examine God's covenantal promises for the believer
- ☛ Explore different examples of people who were healed in the Bible
- ☛ Examine why forgiveness and healing are intertwined
- ☛ Examine the dynamics of growing in relationship with Him
- ☛ Explore the difference between *believing* and *faith*

A covenant is an agreement or promise between to people or parties. God has made an everlasting covenant with us, His children. We are promised a life of walking in the supernatural abundance of provision from the Lord's plenty! We are promised a life of healing, wholeness, and miracles! In this lesson we will continue to strengthen and reinforce our biblical foundation of faith for healing. We will examine the covenant that Father God made with His kids!

_____

_____

_____

_____

_____

_____

_____

_____

_____

_____

_____

_____

_____

_____

_____

_____

_____

_____

_____

_____

KEY SCRIPTURE PASSAGES

I will make you exceedingly fruitful, and I will make nations of you, and kings will come forth from you. I will establish My covenant between Me and you and your descendants after you throughout their generations for an everlasting covenant, to be God to you and to your descendants after you (Gen. 17:6-7).

Christ redeemed us from the curse of the Law, having become a curse for us—for it is written, "Cursed is everyone who hangs on a tree"—in order that in Christ Jesus the blessing of Abraham might come to the Gentiles, so that we would receive the promise of the Spirit through faith (Gal. 3:13-14).

Who forgives all your iniquities, who heals all your diseases (Ps. 103:3, NKJV).

He Himself bore our sins in His body on the cross, so that we might die to sin and live to righteousness; for by His wounds you were healed (1 Peter 2:24).

But He was pierced through for our transgressions, He was crushed for our iniquities; the chastening for our well-being fell upon Him, and by His scourging we are healing (Isa. 53:5).

I. EXAMINING GOD'S COVENANTAL PROMISES FOR THE BELIEVER

A. God's Everlasting Covenant with Abraham for all of his descendants to be fruitful, blessed, and prosperous (Gen. 17:6-8)

B. The Blessing of Abraham comes upon us, the believer; the Promise of the Holy Spirit (Gal. 3:13-14).

C. God has already blessed us with every spiritual blessing in heavenly places in Christ (Eph. 1:3).

D. God promises to prosper us and give us more than we could ever hope, think, or imagine, beyond our wildest dreams! God loves abundance!

   1. Jer. 29:11

   2. Eph. 3:20

   3. John 1:2

E. We are the head and not the tail, above and not beneath (Deut. 28:13).

F. God's covenantal promise for total and complete healing by the shed blood of Jesus Christ

   1. Isa. 53:5

   2. Ps. 103:3

   3. Ps. 147:3

   4. 1 Peter 2:24

G. God's promise for deliverance and freedom from sin, curse, the law, sickness, and disease—complete and total freedom!

    1. John 8:36

    2. Rom. 10:9

H. God promises total salvation!

    1. Eph. 2:8

    2. Rom. 10:9

I. Abundant and eternal life

    1. John 3:16

    2. John 10:10

J. You are called to be an overcomer and more than a conqueror in Christ and with Christ. You conquer sickness with Him!

    1. Rom. 8:37

    2. 1 John 4:4

II. HEALING FUNDAMENTALS

A. Getting Started

    1. Do you want to be made well? (John 5:6)

    2. Do you *believe* Jesus is able to heal you? (Matt. 9:28)

B. Faith is more than belief.

    1. Faith is Action (Acts 14:8-10; James 2:26)

    2. Faith is Expectation (Mark 2:3-5)

C. Forgiveness and healing are intertwined and interconnected. The same blood that washes away your sins is the same blood that heals your body. If you can believe that Jesus is your Savior, start believing He is your Healer, too.

    1. Mark 2:8-11

    2. Ps. 103:3

D. A Re-emphasis on Calvary's Covenant

    1. Isa. 53:5

    2. 1 Peter. 2:24

REFLECTION QUESTIONS

1. What was God's covenantal promise to Abraham and his descendants?

    _____

    _____

2. Why and how does the promise of Abraham come upon us?

    _____

    _____

3. What does abundant life in Christ look like?

    _____

    _____

4. Christ's Kingdom is all about abundant life. What does the enemy's kingdom look like? What does he try to do?

    _____

    _____

5. Do you want to be made well? Do you think people want to be made well? Explain below.

    _____

    _____

6. Do you believe Jesus is able to heal you? Do you believe He will use you to heal the sick?

    _____

    _____

7. What's the difference between belief and faith? What are some characteristics of faith?

_____

_____

8. What is Calvary's covenant with us? How are forgiveness and healing intertwined?

_____

_____

Life Application

In this lesson, we talked about the covenant God made with us through Calvary to forgive all of our sins and to heal all of our disease. It is important to not only believe this, but to also begin activating it by faith in your life. Get before the Lord and ask the Holy Spirit to release His healing power in your life and to direct you on how to release it—for your own healing, for a friend or family member, or for taking it to the streets. After the Holy Spirit shows you… do it!

Prayer

Father God, I thank you for the covenant you cut with me through the shedding of Christ's precious blood. I thank you that in the blood there is not only forgiveness of sins, but healing for every sickness, disease, and affliction. I ask that you would give me a greater revelation of Jesus as Healer and of the abundance of healing power I have backing my every word, prayer, and declaration. Use me to release your healing power in my body, in my family, among my friends, at work, and in the marketplace. In Jesus' name, Amen!

LESSON FIVE
why miracles happen

LESSON OBJECTIVES

☞ Examine various reasons why miracles happen

☞ Identify the purpose for Jesus' miracle ministry in the earth

☞ Explain how you can activate God's miracle and healing power in your life

Compiled in this lesson is a simple list of points that reveal why miracles happen. This is not an exhaustive list, but each point is extremely powerful to help activate God's healing power in your life. Jesus is our ultimate example for the healing and miracle ministry, so take time to meditate on each scripture reference and soak up each revelation to use when ministering in healing and miracles.

_____

_____

_____

_____

_____

_____

_____

_____

_____

_____

_____

_____

_____

_____

_____

_____

_____

_____

KEY SCRIPTURE PASSAGES

The Son of God appeared for this purpose, to destroy the works of the devil (1 John 3:8).

And a great crowd was following Him [Jesus] because they had seen the signs (miracles) which He [continually] performed upon those who were sick (John 6:2, AMP, emphasis added).

Therefore I say to you, all things for which you pray and ask, believe that you have received them, and they will be granted you (Mark 11:24).

When He went ashore, he saw a large, and felt compassion for them and healed their sick (Matt. 14:14).

I. GOD'S LOVE

   A. Moved with compassion (Matt. 14:14)

   B. God gave His only Son because of His great love for us (John 3:16)

   C. Faith working through love (Galatians 5:6)

II. GOD KEEPS HIS WORD

   A. He is a God of Covenant

      1. See Lesson 4: The Assurance of Covenant Healing.

    2. God's Covenant with Abraham (Gen. 17:6-8)

    3. God swore by Himself (Heb. 6:13)

B. God is bound by His Word—He doesn't lie!

    1. Rom. 3:4

    2. Titus 1:2

C. The provision of His Word: *By His stripes I'm healed* (1 Peter 2:24)

III. GOD WILLS IT… HE WANTS TO HEAL (MATT. 8:2-3,6,7).

IV. GOD IS SOVEREIGN… HE DOES WHATEVER HE PLEASES (PS. 115:3; 135:6).

V. MASS EVANGELISM! WE'RE AFTER SOULS AND DISCIPLESHIP!

A. Crowds followed Jesus (Matt 4:24-25).

B. Crowds followed Jesus (John 6:2).

VI. DEMONSTRATION OF DEITY AND BELIEF IN JESUS

A. Mark 2:5-13

B. John 2:11; 1411

VII. FULFILL THE PROPHETIC WORD

A. Isa. 53:3-5

B. Refers to Isa. 53 (Matt. 8:16-17)

VIII. FAITH ATTRACTS THE MIRACULOUS

A. Prayer of Faith (James 5:15)

B. Believe first *and then* receive (Mark 11:24)

C. Faith of the sick person

    1. Matt. 9:22

    2. Matt. 9:27-29

    3. Luke 17:19

D. Another person's faith

    1. Matt. 8:13

    2. John 4:50

IX. AN ANOINTING FOR HEALING

A. And the power of the Lord was present to heal (Luke 5:17)

B. Healing power released (Luke 6:19)

X. PROVE THE MINISTRY

A. The words that you speak are true (1 Kings 17:17-24)

B. God proved Jesus ministry by miracles, signs, and wonders (Acts 2:22)

XI. HE IS RISEN

A. He is alive forevermore (Rev. 1:18)

B. Jesus is the same yesterday, today, and forever (Heb. 13:8)

C. Resurrection of the dead (1 Cor. 15)

XII. HEALING COMMISSION

A. Greater works (John 14:12)

B. He who believes (Mark 16:17-18)

C. Preach the Kingdom and Heal the sick (Matt. 10:1, 7-8)

XIII. REPENTANCE

A. Miracles draw a line in the spirit. They force people to choose: either to repent and believe or to push the truth away. It's one way or the other—white or black, no gray (Matt. 11:21-23).

_____
_____
_____
_____
_____
_____
_____
_____
_____
_____
_____
_____
_____
_____
_____
_____
_____
_____
_____
_____
_____
_____

B. Some people repent and believe; others don't (Ps. 78:12-17)

XIV. SO THAT WE MIGHT BELIEVE

A. John 11:3-5,15

B. John 20:30-31

XV. GOD'S GOODNESS (MATT. 7:7-11)

XVI. GOOD DEEDS AND ACTS OF CHARITY

A. Acts of charity (Acts 9:36-40)

B. Prayers and alms ascended as a memorial before God (Acts 10:1-4)

C. Blessed are those who consider the helpless. God will restore their health (Ps. 41:1-3)

XVII. THE GOSPEL

A. The Gospel is the power of God (Rom. 1:16)

B. The Gospel isn't fully preached unless it's with miracles, signs, and wonders (Rom. 15:19)

C. Signs and wonders confirm the Word (Mark 16:19-20)

XVIII. FRIENDSHIP WITH GOD

A. Face to face, like a man speaks to his friend (Exodus 33:11)

B. No longer servants, but friends—so that we may bear fruit (John 15:15-16)

XIX. THE GLORY OF GOD

A. To glorify God (Matt. 15:31)

B. The workings of God displayed through healings and miracles (John 9:3)

XX. REDEEMED FROM THE CURSE: THE BLESSING OF ABRAHAM (GAL. 3:13-14)

XXI. DESPERATION!

A. If I just touch the hem of His garments (Mark. 5:25-34)

B. Jesus doesn't respond to the need, He responds to the cry (Mark 10:46-52)

C. Persistence (Matt. 15:21-28)

XXII. TO DESTROY THE WORKS OF THE DEVIL

A. Acts 10:38

B. 1 John 3:8

XXIII. THE NAME OF GOD: JEHOVAH RAPHA (EX. 15:26)

XXIV. IN AND BY THE NAME OF JESUS (ACTS 3:6-7)

XXV. GIFTS OF THE SPIRIT—GIFTS OF HEALING (1 COR. 12:9)

XXVI. THE SPIRIT OF GOD

A. Creative power in His brooding presence (Gen. 1:2)

B. The indwelling presence of the Holy Spirit gives life to our mortal bodies (Rom. 8:11)

XXVII. KINGDOM

A. God's will is His Kingdom established and manifested on earth as it is in heaven (Matt. 6:10)

B. Casting out demons is advancing the Kingdom (Matt. 12:28)

REFLECTION QUESTIONS

1. Healing power flows through love and compassion. Who demonstrated this? Why do you think this happens?

   _____

   _____

2. Try, by memory, to list eight of the 27 listed reasons why God heals.

   _____

   _____

3. In a couple sentences, explain one of those eight points below.

   _____

   _____

4. Explain another one of those eight points below.

   _____

   _____

5. How do you know you are commissioned to heal the sick?

   _____

   _____

6. Why is the healing and miracle ministry so important for evangelism?

   _____

   _____

7.   What did Paul say about *fully* preaching the Gospel?

_____

_____

8.   Paraphrase a Scripture verse from this lesson that impacted you deeply.

_____

_____

Life Application

In this lesson, we talked about reasons miracles and healings happen and how to activate God's healing power in your life. Get alone with God and scan back over one specific point in this lesson that really impacted you deeply. Open your Bible and meditate on those verses. Ask the Holy Spirit to remove any blinders or lies that would try to keep you from receiving a full revelation of God's healing power and His desire to heal everyone. Ask Him to reveal how He wants you to apply this lesson to your daily life so that you can be more like Jesus in heart, mind, and action. Write down whatever He shows you and do what He says…. You might be surprised at what happens!

Prayer

Father God, I thank you that it's your desire to not only save all people, but to heal them as well. I thank you for giving me a large arsenal in this lesson of why miracles happen, and the things I can do to activate your healing power in my life. I ask that you would use me daily in the healing ministry to speak words of encouragement, to lay hands on the sick and see them recover, to set the captives free, and to love people with your uncreated, eternal, unconditional love. Use me, in Jesus' name, Amen!

LESSON SIX
the working of faith and an atmosphere for miracles

LESSON OBJECTIVES

☛ Examine the five levels of faith

☛ Examine different types of faith including the gift of faith and the measure of faith

☛ Examine the healing anointing and the gifts of healing and miracles

☛ Discover the difference between personal and corporate anointings and atmospheres

In this lesson, we'll examine the five levels of faith, the different types of faith, and how to move in faith to activate the healing and miracle gifts. We'll also discuss how to use your personal gifts and atmosphere to influence and change the corporate atmosphere. Bring the possibilities of heaven into impossible situations.

KEY SCRIPTURE PASSAGES

Then the disciples came to Jesus privately and said, "Why could we not drive it out?" And He said to them, "Because of the littleness of your faith; for truly I say to you, if you have faith the size of a mustard seed, you will say to this mountain, 'Move from here to there,' and it will move; and nothing will be impossible to you" (Matt. 17:19-20).

*Now when Jesus heard this, he marveled and said to those who were following, "Truly I say to you, I have not found such **great faith** with anyone in Israel"* (Matt. 8:10).

For in the Gospel a righteousness which God ascribes is revealed, both springing from faith and leading to faith [disclosed through the way of faith that arouses to more faith]. As it is written, The man who through faith is just and upright shall live and shall live by faith (Rom. 1:17 AMP).

*But to each one is given the manifestation of the Spirit for the common good. …to another faith by the same Spirit, and to another **gifts** of healing by one Spirit, and to another the effecting of miracles…* (1 Cor. 12:7, 9-10).

…God has allotted to each a measure of faith (Rom. 12:3).

So faith comes from hearing, and hearing by the word of Christ (Rom. 10:17).

I. FIVE LEVELS OF FAITH

A. No Faith (Mark 4:40; James 2:17) and total unbelief (Mark 6:5-6)

B. Little Faith (Matt. 14:31; Matt. 8:26)

C. Faith (Matt. 9:29; Luke 5:20)

D. Strong Faith (Rom. 4:20)

E. Great Faith (Matt. 8:10; Matt. 15:28)

II. TYPES OF FAITH

A. The Measure of Faith

    1. By His grace He has given each man a measure of faith (Rom. 12:3; Eph. 4:7).

    2. Faith to move mountains (Matt. 17:19-20)

    3. Whatever you ask for in faith, you will receive (Matt. 21:21-22)

    4. A seed that grows (Mark 4:30-32)

    5. Faith comes by hearing (Rom. 10:17).

B. The Gift of Faith

    1. A Gift of Faith is different than a measure of faith (1 Cor. 12:7-9).

    2. Grace received through faith (Eph. 2:8)

C. The Faith that is Ever-Increasing

1. From Faith to Faith (Rom. 1:17)

2. Increase our Faith! (Luke 17:5)

III. PERSONAL AND CORPORATE GIFTS, ANOINTINGS, AND ATMOSPHERES

A. Gifts of Healings and Miracles—Personal Anointings and Atmospheres

   1. "Gifts" of healing is plural… with an "s" (1 Cor. 12:7-11).

   2. Earnestly desire gifts; pursue, lust after them (1 Cor. 12:31; 1 Cor. 14:1).

   3. The anointing in you (1 John 2:20, 27)

B. Corporate Anointings, Faith, The Power of the Lord Present to Heal

   1. In a corporate setting, using your gifts to work healings and miracles increases people's faith, paving the way for greater releases of power.

      a) Gifts of the Holy Spirit—miracles, signs and wonders (Heb. 2:4)

      b) Gift of faith/healing (James 5:14)

      c) Gifts of healing and miracles (Acts 8:6-13)

      d) Gift of Faith/Miracles (Acts 3:16)

e) While ministering in a corporate setting, I'll begin to minister out of a
miracle or healing gift—this brings the
anointing. From there, I'll minister under the anointing. When people begin
to see all the miracles, they praise the
Lord and give Him Glory—their faith
levels rise. Faith and high praise will
usher in a greater Glory and anointing,
creating an ideal atmosphere for greater
miracles. As the people's expectation increases, so do the miracles!

2. Your personal anointing affects the atmosphere, spilling over onto others. You bring
an atmosphere with you that clashes against
all other atmospheres.

   a) Peter's shadow heals the sick
   (Acts 5:15).

   b) Jesus anointed to heal the sick and cast
   out demons (Acts 10:38)

3. The Glory comes and the power of God is
present to heal. This isn't a gift of faith, a
gift for healing or miracles, or even a healing
anointing—this is the tangible presence of
the Lord.

   a) The power of the Lord present to heal
   (Luke 5:17)

_____

_____

_____

_____

_____

_____

_____

_____

_____

_____

_____

_____

_____

_____

_____

_____

_____

_____

b) Jesus healed them all (Matt. 12:15-16).

c) Many don't understand this, but there is a difference between the anointing and the Glory. In the anointing, healings occur, but it's more on an individual level. Through a gift of healing or the working of power, the minister prays for someone, and they're healed. Then, moving to the next, he prays, they're healed, and so on. The minister is operating in the healing anointing, which covers him like a mantle, and he releases it to the people.

The Glory cloud, however, is completely different. It's like a covering or a canopy that blankets the people—they *all* get touched. When the cloud of Glory is present, there is direct contact with heaven—revelation increases, the seer realm is opened, gifts are activated, and miracles happen all over. There are many things being said about the Glory of God, so I want to make sure I define it as clearly as I possibly can. The Glory of God is the manifest presence and person of the Lord Jesus Christ. It's that simple. In the presence of God there is limitless abundance for everything we have need of: creative miracles, revelation, power, etc. The children of Israel were a generation fed, nourished, and protected in the wilderness by the cloud of Glory, for it was His presence that went with them. This new Glory Generation will be marked by the presence of God!

REFLECTION QUESTIONS

1. What are the five levels of faith?

_____

_____

2. What is the gift of faith?

_____

_____

3. How does faith come?

_____

_____

4. Can your faith for miracles increase? What can you do to increase your faith?

_____

_____

5. Why couldn't Jesus do many miracles in His hometown?

_____

_____

6. Why is "gifts" of healing plural in 1 Corinthians 12:7-11? Are we allowed to pursue the best gifts and graces? Explain why below.

_____

_____

7. What does it mean to carry your own atmosphere of the presence of God? What are some ways you can increase God's daily presence in your life?

_____

_____

8. What's the difference between the anointing and the Glory?

_____

_____

Life Application

Grab your journal and Bible, and get alone with God. Read Mathew 8:5-10,13 slowly a couple times. Ask the Holy Spirit to release a revelation of the authority in the spoken word that is accessed through great faith. Stay in the presence and ask for the Holy Spirit to release to you the gift of faith for healings and miracles. Many of you will receive or already have received this gift of faith. Journal anything the Holy Spirit speaks to you during your time with Him. It's important to access the gift of faith immediately—find a sick person you can pray for. This could be a relative, friend, someone in your church, etc. Trust the Holy Spirit to give you the words—move and pray in faith. Take time to wait on the Lord, too. But continue praying....

Prayer

Father God, thank you for a fresh impartation of faith. Lord, increase my faith for healings and miracles to flow in my life! I'm asking you for the gift of faith to be activated. Thank you for a fresh healing anointing that's going to overflow and spill out everywhere I go. Thank you for the deaf ears that are popping open! Thank you for the blind eyes that can now see! Thank you for healing back problems, sore knees, and headaches in the name of Jesus Christ! Teach me how to follow the Spirit of God and release your healing power—faith through love. Use me not only in the nations, but also during my daily routine—at work, school, and at home. Jesus, to You be all Glory, Honor, and Power! In Your precious name, Amen.

LESSON SEVEN
the ministry of creative miracles

LESSON OBJECTIVES

☞ Examine creative miracles from the beginning

☞ Learn the difference between healings, miracles, signs, and wonders

☞ Learn about God as Creator and you being made in His image

☞ Learn about the creative power for miracles in you

☞ Discover the power of the spoken word

God is Creator and we were made in His image. We were born to create—it's in our DNA because we came from His DNA! We have the creative nature and Spirit of God living inside of us, giving us power to not only heal the sick, but also to perform creative miracles! Sorcerers, witches, and followers of New Age have nothing on a Spirit filled believer—the same Spirit that raised Jesus from the dead lives in you! In this lesson, we will examine several keys for accessing and releasing God's creative miracle power in your life!

————————————
————————————
————————————
————————————
————————————
————————————
————————————
————————————
————————————
————————————
————————————
————————————
————————————
————————————
————————————
————————————
————————————
————————————
————————————
————————————
————————————
————————————

KEY SCRIPTURE PASSAGES

Then the LORD said to Moses, "See, I make you as God to Pharaoh…" (Ex. 7:1).

The earth was without form and an empty waste, and darkness was upon the face of the very great deep. The Spirit of God was moving (hovering, brooding) over the face of the waters. And God said… (Gen. 1:2-3, AMP).

But if the Spirit of Him who raise Jesus from the dead dwells in you, He who raised Christ Jesus from the dead will also give life to your mortal bodies through His Spirit who dwells in you (Rom. 8:11).

When it was evening, the disciples came to Him and said, "This place is desolate and the hour is already late; so send the crowds away, that they may go into the villages and buy food for themselves." But Jesus said to them, "They do not need to go away; you give them something to eat!" They said to Him, "We have here only five loaves and two fish." And He said, "Bring them here to Me." Ordering the people to sit down on the grass, He took the five loaves and the two fish, and looking up toward heaven, He blessed the food, and breaking the loaves He gave them to the disciples, and the disciples gave them to the crowds, and they all ate and were satisfied. They picked up what was left over of the broken pieces, twelve full baskets. There were about five thousand men who ate, besides women and children (Matt. 14:15-21).

I. CREATIVE MIRACLES IN THE BEGINNING

A. The Spirit of God brooding, hovering, and moving—then the spoken word (Gen. 1:1-3)

B. Spirit creates (Ps. 104:30)

II. THE DIFFERENCE BETWEEN HEALINGS, MIRACLES, SIGNS, AND WONDERS

A. Healing

    1. They will recover over time: a few minutes or days, but not instantly (Mark 16:17-18)

    2. Walking out your healing; as you go (Luke 17:11-19)

B. Miracle

    1. Instant manifestation (Mark 2:10-12; 7:32-35)

    2. A creative miracle is when something is produced from nothing or when something is multiplied (e.g. an eyeball growing back into the socket, a leg growing out, an eardrum being recreated, etc)

C. Signs & Wonders

    1. Heavenly wonders in the sky above and signs on the earth below (Acts 2:19)

_____

_____

_____

_____

_____

_____

_____

_____

_____

_____

_____

_____

_____

_____

_____

_____

_____

_____

_____

_____

_____

2. Time stands still (Josh. 10:13)

3. Parting the Red Sea and all the other signs Moses performed in Egypt (Ex. 14:13-22)

4. Miracles are actually signs and wonders too, because it's supernatural—signs point to Jesus. Some *miracles* are actually *signs* that make you *wonder!* Some examples: Manna from heaven (Ex. 16:4; Ps. 78:25), water into wine (John 2:1-11), and unusual miracles worked at the hands of Paul (Acts 19:11-12).

5. Other signs and wonders that we've experienced are gems falling during worship, gold dust and angel feathers manifesting, gold fillings and gold teeth, water turning into wine, and manna coming in meetings! These are all signs that point to Jesus—we shouldn't put Him in a box! He does whatever He wants! (Ps. 115:3)

III. CREATOR GOD—YOU ARE MADE IN HIS IMAGE

A. God is Elohim—Creator God. In the beginning God created... (Gen. 1:1)

B. You are made in His image and likeness. You were made to create (Gen. 1:26-27).

C. We are like God to this Pharaoh [the Earth] (Ex. 7:1).

D. God wants to use our hands to perform creative miracles (Matt.14:15-21)

E. Authority over the natural realm [weather] (Mark 4:39)

F. Ye are gods!

    1. Ps. 82:6-8

    2. John 10:34

IV. CREATIVE POWER IN YOU!

A. The Spirit who raised Jesus from the dead lives in you (Rom. 8:11)

B. Christ is Creator and He lives in you (John 1:1-5; Col. 1:27)

C. You are born of God—God's imperishable seed in you gives you power over sin and the devil (1 John 3:8-9; 1 Peter 1:23)

D. God's anointing abides in you (1 John 1:27)

E. The Kingdom within—tapping into heavenly resources inside (Luke17:21)

F. Rivers of living water

    1. John 4:14

    2. John 7:38

V. THE POWER OF THE SPOKEN WORD

A. Death and life are in the power of the tongue (Prov. 18:21)

B. Creative Speaking, Decreeing, and Declaring

    1. Calls into being that which does not exist (Rom. 4:17)

    2. Called into being by the prophetic word (Isa. 48:7, AMP)

C. Speak the Word (Matt. 8:5-13)

D. The Principle of Multiplication

    1. 5,000 fed (Matt. 14:15-21)

    2. At Elijah's word the jar of oil and bowl of flour were not exhausted (1 Kings 17:8-16).

    3. At Elisha's word all the pots were supernatural filled (2 Kings 4:1-7)

REFLECTION QUESTIONS

1. After looking at Genesis 1 and John 1, what are some key components necessary for creative power to be released?

    _____

    _____

2. What's the difference between a healing and a miracle?

    _____

    _____

3. What exactly is a creative miracle?

    _____

    _____

4. What are signs and wonders? What are their purposes?

    _____

    _____

5. How does being made in the image of God give you the ability to move in creative power?

    _____

    _____

6. What does it mean that the Kingdom of heaven, the anointing, and God's seed are in you? What do you have access to?

    _____

    _____

7. What are some reasons creative miracles are available to you?

_____

_____

8. Why is it important to understand the power that resides within the spoken word?

_____

_____

Life Application

Get with a partner and review this lesson with them. Pray for them to receive a revelation of "Christ in you the hope of glory," and other things as you feel led by the Spirit. Pray for activation and a release of creative miracles in their life. Then, find somebody who needs a creative miracle and get to it! Journal anything the Lord does or shows you!

Prayer

Father God, I ask that You would give me a revelation of Christ in me the hope of glory—a revelation of the Kingdom within, the anointing within, and God's seed growing within my spirit man. Teach me how to live and walk in your Kingdom, and let creative miracles begin to pop open in my life. I thank You for Your saving, healing, and miracle power on my life. I ask that You would give me opportunity to walk in Your creative power. Increase my faith so that I see a release and demonstration of Kingdom power and glory. I worship you, praise you, and give all the glory to You, in Jesus' precious name, Amen!

LESSON EIGHT
why miracles don't happen

LESSON OBJECTIVES

- ☛ Examine some reasons why miracles don't happen
- ☛ Identify hindrances blocking the miracle flow in your own life
- ☛ With the Holy Spirit, discover how to remove those hindrances

In this lesson, we'll examine reasons why miracles don't happen—hindrances keeping God's healing and miracle power from flowing in your life and ministry. Many of these reasons are obvious, but several are actually hidden agendas of the enemy that most of the church in America has yet to understand. I want to expose these concealed agendas, and bring to light these hidden hindrances. Once you identify what they really are, with the Holy Spirit, you can begin moving past these hindrances so that the miracle and healing power of God can more effectively flow.

_____
_____
_____
_____
_____
_____
_____
_____
_____
_____
_____
_____
_____
_____
_____
_____
_____
_____

OPENING PRAYER

Holy Spirit, I ask that as I go through this lesson you would grant me a spirit of understanding— I want to see clearly these hindrances that keep me, and the church as a whole, from moving in a greater flow of Your miracle and healing power. I invite you to come have Your way in my heart, my mind, and my entire life. Show me how to function and flow in the healing and miracle gifts and anointings in a greater capacity, in Jesus' name, Amen!

I. LITTLE FAITH

A. You of little faith (Matt. 8:26)

B. Little faith, doubt (Matt. 14:31)

II. UNBELIEF

A. Mark 6:1, 5-6

B. Perverted and unbelieving generation (Matt. 17:17)

III. UNFORGIVENESS

A. Matt. 6:14-15

B. Matt. 5:23-24

C. Matt. 18:34-35

IV. SIN

A. John 5:14

B. James 5:16

V. DISOBEDIENCE

A. Do what Jesus tells you (John 6:26)

B. 1 Kings 17:11-16

VI. PRIDE

A. 2 Kings 5:10-11

B. He empowers us with His Spirit and grace when we're humble (James 4:5-6)

VII. FEAR

A. What I fear comes upon me (Job 3:25)

B. Perfect Love is the answer for overcoming fear (1 John 4:18)

VIII. ANXIETY, WORRY, AND FEAR

A. Your heart is the wellspring of life (Prov. 4:23)
B. Matt. 6:25-34

C. Phil. 4:6

IX. LACK OF INTIMACY (JOHN 15:5-7)

X. LACK OF PRAYER AND FASTING —PRAYERLESSNESS

A. Matt. 17:21

B. Luke 11:54

C. 2 Tim. 3.5

XI. DEMONS CAUSING SICKNESS

A. Infirmity (Luke 13:10-11)

B. Epilepsy (Matt. 17:14-15)

C. Deaf and dumb (Mark 9:25)

D. Mute (Matt. 9:32-33)

E. Blindness (Matt. 12:22)

F. Depression (Isa. 61:3)

G. All Sicknessis rooted in the devil's kingdom (Acts 10:38)

XII. RELIGIOUS SPIRIT & ATTITUDES

A. Matt. 11:16-19

B. Matt. 16:1

C. Luke 11:54

D. 2 Tim. 3:5

XIII. NO EXPECTATION

A. Acts 3:5

B. James 4:2-3

XIV. UNSCRIPTURAL DOCTRINES (MATT. 22:29)

XV. EXCUSES (JOHN 5:7)

XVI. MOTIVE

A. John 6:26

B. James 4:3

C. 1 John 5:14-15

XVII. COMPLAINING AND MURMURING

A. Num. 21:4-5

B. Ps. 78:18-20, 32-33

XVIII. OUR CONFESSION (WORDS)

A. Prov. 12:14,18

_____

_____

_____

_____

_____

_____

_____

_____

_____

_____

_____

_____

_____

_____

_____

_____

_____

B. Prov. 15:4

C. Prov. 18:20-21

XIX. IGNORANCE (HOS. 4:6)

XX. BROKEN SPIRIT

A. Prov. 17:22

B. Prov. 18:14

XXI. HARDENED HEART

A. Rebellious (Ezek. 12:1-2)

B. Keeps us from seeing and hearing (Mark 8:15-17)

C. Forgetting the working of miracles, signs, and wonders (Ps. 78:8-10)

D. Keeps us for knowing the ways of the Lord (Heb. 3:8-11)

XXII. GREED

A. Simon (Acts 8:18-20)

B. Gehazi (2 Kings 5:15-27)

XXIII. FORGETTING THE POOR

A. Giving ascends to God (Acts 10:1-4)

B. Healing and speedy recovery come after helping the poor (Isa. 58:7-8)

C. Those who shut their ears to the cry of the poor will also cry themselves and not be answered (Prov. 21:13).

XXIV. NEGATIVE INFLUENCE

A. Mark 5:35

B. Luke 18:39

C. 2 Kings 4:23

XXV. NOT KNOWING THE GOODNESS OF GOD

A. Every good and perfect gift—healings and miracles are gifts (James 1:17)

B. Be in good health and prosper in every way (3 John 1:2)

XXVI. LACK OF MARITAL HARMONY (1 PETER 3:7)

XXVII. OFFENDED AT THE VESSEL/OFFENSE

A. Taking offense hinders miracles from flowing (Mark 6:1-6)

B. Blessed is he who doesn't take offense (Luke 7:23)

REFLECTION QUESTIONS

1. What is one story in the Bible where unbelief kept somebody from receiving a miracle?

    _____

    _____

2. There are several consequences from harboring unforgiveness in our hearts. What are a few of those consequences?

    _____

    _____

3. Explain why sin and disobedience hinder miracles and healing from flowing.

    _____

    _____

4. How can a lack of intimacy and fellowship keep God's miracle power from resting on our lives? What parable did Jesus use to explain this?

    _____

    _____

5. What are six specific types of demons that cause sickness?

    _____

    _____

6. Explain what Hosea 4:6 means below.

    _____

    _____

7. Out of all the reasons discussed in this lesson that keep God's miracle power from flowing into and through your life, which one has the greatest influence in your life? What steps do you think you should take to overcome this problem?

_____

_____

8. What is Calvary's covenant with us? How are forgiveness and healing intertwined?

_____

_____

Life Application

Get out your Bible and journal, and find a quiet place to meet with the Lord. Review this lesson, and ask the Holy Spirit to reveal the top five reasons that keep God's miracle and healing power from flowing through your life. Jot these issues down below (If there are more than five, finish the Life Application on a separate sheet of paper). Ask the Holy Spirit what steps you need to take to overcome the issues on your list, and write down what He speaks to your heart (e.g. repenting for sin in your life, forgiving someone, renouncing demonic strongholds in your life, praying through each issue, etc.).

After hearing from the Lord and completing your list, write a prayer from your heart in the space provided in the next section using the strategy you received from the Lord concerning these issues. Pray and write as led by the Holy Spirit.

1. Reason/Issue — Explain Below:

_____

_____

_____

_____

_____

What steps do you feel like the Holy Spirit is directing you to take to move past this?

_____

_____

_____

_____

2. Reason/Issue — Explain Below:

_____

_____

_____

_____

What steps do you feel like the Holy Spirit is directing you to take to move past this?

_____

_____

_____

_____

3.   Reason/Issue — Explain Below:

_____

_____

_____

_____

What steps do you feel like the Holy Spirit is directing you to move past this?

_____

_____

_____

_____

4.   Reason/Issue — Explain Below:

_____

_____

_____

_____

What steps do you feel like the Holy Spirit is directing you to take to move past this?

_____

_____

_____

_____

_____

5. Reason/Issue — Explain Below:

_____

_____

_____

_____

What steps do you feel like the Holy Spirit is directing you to take to move past this?

_____

_____

_____

_____

Prayer

_____

_____

_____

_____

_____

_____

LESSON NINE
total freedom from the roots
of sickness and disease

LESSON OBJECTIVES

☞ Examine the history of sickness and Christ's (our) victory over it

☞ Expose what sickness really is

☞ Discover the difference between suffering and sickness

☞ Learn why genuine humility is key for God's abiding power

☞ Discover how some sickness is rooted in the heart and grows from there

☞ Learn how to strike the root instead of aiming at the fruit

There are many misconceptions currently in the church concerning sickness, persecution, suffering, and discipline. In this lesson, we'll examine the differences between these four topics and then hone in on sickness and how to get rid of it! We'll discover how inward healing often brings outward healing, and why inward wounds sometimes keep a person's body from being completely healed. It's time to strike the root instead of the fruit!

KEY SCRIPTURE PASSAGES

The thief comes only to steal and kill and destroy; I came that they may have life, and have it abundantly (John 10:10).

And He has said to me, "My grace is sufficient for you, for power is perfected in weakness." Most gladly, therefore, I will rather boast about my weaknesses, so that the power of Christ may dwell in me (2 Cor. 12:9).

The spirit of man is the lamp of the LORD, searching all the innermost parts of his being (Prov. 20:27).

Above all else, guard your heart, for it is the wellspring of life (Prov. 4:23).

I. HISTORY OR "HIS" STORY?

A. In the Beginning—The Good News and the Bad News!

    1. Made in God's image (Gen. 1:26-27)

    2. Sin enters (Gen. 3; Rom. 5:12-14)

B. Jesus' Victory over Sickness—The best news!

    1. Free from the law of sin and death (Rom. 8:2-11)

2. By His stripes (Isa. 53:8) _____

C. Jesus as our Role Model _____

    1. Greater Works (John 14:12) _____

    2. The Spirit of the Lord has anointed me… (Luke 4:18) _____

D. The Great Commission _____

    1. He who believes in Me… (Mark 16:15-18) _____

    2. Sent out to preach the Kingdom and bring healing (Luke 9:1-2) _____

E. His Story is our Destiny—We are in Christ _____

    1. Hidden with Christ in God (Col. 3:3) _____

    2. Crucified with Christ (Gal. 2:20) _____

    3. Ascended with Christ into heavenly places (Eph. 2:6) _____

    4. When Christ returns we will appear with Him in Glory (Col. 3:4). _____

II. SEEING SICKNESS FOR WHAT IT IS

A. The Author of Sickness and Disease _____

    1. The thief comes to steal, kill, and destroy (John 10:10) _____

    2. Healing all who are oppressed of the devil (Acts 10:38) _____

B. Sickness, Discipline, and Persecution

  1. Is anyone sick? Let them pray so that they will be healed (James 5:13-15).

  2. Those the Lord loves, He disciplines, corrects, etc. But a loving Father doesn't discipline His child by giving him cancer. We receive correction and discipline from the Lord, but sickness is from the enemy (Heb. 12:5-11)

  3. Those who are in Christ will suffer persecution. Persecution is not sickness (2 Tim. 3:12)

C. Job's Trials

  1. Satan smote Job with sores, not God (Job. 2:7)

  2. Fear opens a door to the enemy (Job 3:25)

D. Paul's Thorn (2 Cor. 12:7-10 AMP)

  1. A thorn/splinter is something small causing irritation

  2. To buffet means to strike repeatedly. This can't be sickness otherwise it would be one sickness after another.

  3. *"I will show him how great things he must suffer for My name's sake"* (Acts 9:16 KJV). The suffering and buffeting Paul went through were persecutions and outward circumstances, not physical sickness.

4. God said that His grace was sufficient for Paul. The "grace" of God was inward power to overcome outward circumstances. Humility is key for God's abiding power to rest on you.

III. STRIKING THE ROOT—GETTING TO THE HEART OF THE MATTER

A. The parts/rooms of your heart

1. Healing and life in the center of the heart release healing into the body (Prov. 4:22)

2. *Innermost Parts* or *inner depths* of the body (Prov. 20:30)

3. What happens in your body is linked to the heart. As you think/believe in your heart, so is your body and life (Prov. 23:7)

B. Guard your heart

1. From it flows all of heaven (Prov. 4:23)

2. Keep your heart at peace—then it will bring life to your body (Prov. 14:30)

C. Don't give place to the devil (Eph. 4:27)

D. What springs from the inside can defile (Mark. 7:20-23)

E. Heart Problems

    1. Unforgiveness (Matt. 18:21-35)

    2. Offense

        a) Keeps someone from hearing the truth (Prov. 18:19)

        b) Reconciliation is key (Matt. 5:23-24)

    3. Envy (Prov. 14:30)

    4. Pride (2 Kings 5:9-11)

    5. Lust

        a) Prov. 2:16-19

        b) Prov. 5:1-4

        c) Matt. 5:28

    6. Self-Hatred

        a) Love yourself as you love others (Mark 12:33)

        b) Moved past self-hatred to a demonic root, causing a deeper level of self-hatred/suicide/rage, etc. (Mark 9:17-27)

    7. Rebellion (1 Sam. 15:23)

    8. Greed (Prov. 1:19)

9. Not discerning the Lord's body
(1 Cor. 11:27-30)

F. Merry, Sorrowful, and Broken Hearts

   1. Merry heart (Prov. 17:22)

   2. Sorrowful/Anxious Heart (Prov. 12:25)

   3. Broken spirit (Prov. 15:13; Prov. 17:22)

G. Pleasant and Unpleasant Words

   1. Pleasant healing words (Prov. 16:24)

   2. Unpleasant, Wounding, and evil Words
   (Prov. 18:8, 20-21)

H. Revelation, healing, and miracles flow from the
heart (spirit man).

   1. The spirit of man is God's lamp
   (Prov. 20:27).

   2. The Kingdom within (Luke 17:21)

   3. Christ in you…

      a) The hope of Glory (Col. 1:27)

      b) Dwells in your heart through faith
      (Eph. 3:17)

   4. The Holy Spirit within (1 Cor. 2:4-16)

REFLECTION QUESTIONS

1. Why do we have victory over sickness?

    _____

    _____

2. What does it mean to be free from sin and death?

    _____

    _____

3. Explain below what it means to be seated in heavenly places.

    _____

    _____

4. Who causes sickness? What verse(s) in the Bible support this?

    _____

    _____

5. Who heals sickness? What verse(s) in the Bible support this?

    _____

    _____

6. What is one major key for God's power to rest and abide in you and on you? Explain why below.

    _____

    _____

7. Can an inner heart issue keep someone from receiving a full physical healing? Explain this below.

_____

_____

8. Explain what Proverbs 20:27 means below.

_____

_____

Life Application

Get alone with the Holy Spirit and review the heart issues mentioned above. Ask the Holy Spirit for wisdom about these issues and how He can lead/move you past them (e.g. repentance, forgiving someone, breaking soul ties and word curses, etc.). Do anything the Holy Spirit leads you to do, and journal anything He shows you. If you need a physical healing in your body that hasn't manifested yet, ask the Lord to heal you.

Prayer

Father God, I thank You for Your love and care, and for the revelation that you do not cause sickness or disease. I thank You for revealing that the enemy causes sickness and that we have victory over all sickness and disease through the shed blood of Jesus Christ. I ask that you would teach me how to strike at the root instead of the fruit. I ask that You would come heal every broken place in my heart and show me who I need to forgive. Lead me into a place of total freedom and healing internally and externally, in Jesus' name.

LESSON TEN
maintaining your healing

LESSON OBJECTIVES

☞ Examine why people sometimes lose their healing

☞ Discover the four principles of keeping your spiritual house in order

☞ Examine three major keys for maintaining your healing

On occasion, after a person receives a healing or miracle in their physical body, the problem will come back a short time after. These people were undoubtedly touched by the power of God, yet why is it their infirmity or pain returned? In this lesson, we'll examine why people sometimes lose their healing. We'll discover some ways to keep your spiritual house clean and occupied by the Holy Spirit, then we'll examine several vital keys for not only maintaining your healing, but also living completely free from all sickness and all disease.

KEY SCRIPTURE PASSAGES

The sower sows the word. These are the ones who are beside the road where the word is sown; and when they hear, immediately Satan comes and takes away the word which has been sown in them. In a similar way these are the ones on whom seed was sown on the rocky places, who, when they hear the word, immediately receive it with joy; and they have no firm root in themselves, but are only temporary; then, when affliction or persecution arises because of the word, immediately they fall away. And others are the ones on whom seed was sown among the thorns; these are the ones on whom seed was sown among the thorns; these are the ones who have heard the word, but the worries of the world, and the deceitfulness of riches, and the desires for other things enter in and choke the word, and it becomes unfruitful. And those are the ones on whom seed was sown on the good soil; and they hear the word and accept it and bear fruit, thirty, sixty, and a hundredfold (Mark 4:14-20).

Then it says, "I will return to my house from which I came"; and when it comes, it finds it unoccupied, swept, and put in order. Then it goes and takes along with it seven other spirits more wicked than itself, and they go in and live there; and the last state of that man becomes worse than the first. That is the way it will also be with this evil generation (Matt. 12:44-45).

And they overcame him because of the blood of the Lamb and because of the word of their testimony, and they did not love their life even when faced with death (Rev. 12:11).

I. WAYS PEOPLE SOMETIMES LOSE THEIR HEALING

The sower sows the word. These are the ones who are beside the road where the word is sown; and when they hear, **(A)** *immediately Satan comes and takes away the word* *which has been sown in them. In a similar way these are the ones on whom seed was sown on the rocky places, who, when they hear the word,* **(B)** *immediately receive it with joy; and they have no firm root in themselves, but are only temporary; then, when affliction or persecution arises because of the word, immediately they fall away.* *And others are the ones on whom seed was sown among the thorns; these are the ones on whom seed was sown among the thorns;* **(C)** *these are the ones who have heard the word, but the worries of the world, and the deceitfulness of riches, and the desires for other things enter in and choke the word, and it becomes unfruitful.* *And those are the ones on whom seed was sown on the good soil; and* **(D)** *they hear the word and accept it and bear fruit, thirty, sixty, and a hundredfold* (Mark 4:14-20).

In the parable of the sower, the soil represents the *heart of the person,* and the seed that is sown represents the *Word of the Kingdom.* The Word of the Kingdom involves God's healing power, and, as we already know, healings and miracles are part of the preaching of the Kingdom of God—the sowing of the Word into the hearts of men.

119

_____

_____

_____

_____

_____

_____

_____

_____

_____

_____

_____

_____

_____

_____

_____

_____

_____

_____

A. This shows us that sometimes, immediately after a person is healed the, enemy comes forth and snatches it back. The person who has received the healing didn't do anything wrong—it is simply the enemy's nature to snatch away the full manifestation of the Kingdom promise.

B. This shows us a person who wants a healing but is unwilling to stop walking in disobedience or the very thing that opened a door and brought the sickness in the first place (e.g. smoking causes lung cancer; a lack of learning to walk in rest causes a weak immune system, which invites sickness; negative word curses like "I'm sick and tired of…" actually cause you to become sick and tired; etc.). Oftentimes, they have one foot in God and one foot in the world. We need to do as Jesus said and "…*go and sin no more*" (John 8:11 NKJV).

C. This shows us a person who receives their healing but allows worries, fears, and doubts to sneak in and choke the healing. This represents the lies and deceitfulness of the enemy that open up all types of doors for sickness. *Desires for other things* represent other methods for being healed including therapy, medication, surgery, etc. Though these things aren't bad in themselves, they are harmful when rooted in doubt and unbelief in God's healing power.

D. This shows a person who receives a healing or miracle in their physical body—one who keeps it by closing all open doors to the enemy, by staying in a place of faith and belief, and by continually being filled with the Holy Spirit, etc.

II. KEEPING YOUR HOUSE OCCUPIED... WITH THE RIGHT SPIRIT!

Now when the unclean spirit goes out of a man, it passes through waterless places seeking rest, and does not find it. Then it says, "I will return to my house from which I came"; and when it comes, it finds it unoccupied, swept, and put in order. Then it goes and takes along with it seven other spirits more wicked than itself, and they go in and live there; and the last state of that man becomes worse than the first. That is the way it will also be with this evil generation." (Matt. 12:43-45).

Once somebody is healed or delivered from a particular sickness that was brought on by a demonic spirit, there's a possibility that the problem will come back—and even greater—if the person isn't filled/refilled with the Holy Spirit, revelation, anointing, Word, etc. Our bodies/hearts have several rooms: we are the temples of the Holy Spirit. When someone is healed and a room is cleaned, it's important to fill that empty space with the Holy Spirit and everything He brings. If not, it's likely the sickness/demon will return and the outcome will be worse than before.

A. Read and meditate on the Word. Meditation brings revelation, and revelation brings a manifestation.

_____

1. Don't depart from the Word; it's health to your body (Prov. 4:20-22)

2. Scripture is inspired by God (2 Timothy 3:16)

B. Worship, Praise, Thanksgiving: Creating your atmosphere

1. High Praise and the double-sided sword (Ps.149:5-6)

2. Thanksgiving and thinking on good things (Phil. 4:6-9)

C. Guard against the deception of the enemy

1. The devil prowls like a lion looking for someone to devour (1 Peter 5:8-9)

2. The armor of God (Eph. 6:10-18)

3. Don't give the devil a foothold (Eph. 4:27)

D. Continual infilling with the Holy Spirit. This verse can be translated, "...*be, being filled*," as in a continual infilling, not a onetime event (Eph. 6:10-18).

III. KEYS FOR KEEPING YOUR HEALING AND LIVING FREE FROM ALL SICKNESS AND DISEASE

A. Three Powerful Keys (Rev. 12:11)

    1. The Blood of the Lamb

    2. The Word of Your Testimony

    3. Not loving your life even to death

B. Understand that sickness and disease is from Satan, not from God (you should know this by now!).

    1. John 10:10

    2. Acts 10:38

C. Appreciate the Wonder-working Power of God and ONLY BELIEVE!

    1. Believe before you see!

        a) John 4:48

        b) John 20:29

    2. Take Him at His Word (Matt.38-39)

    3. Appreciate the miracles and wonders, don't forget them (Ps. 77:11-15)

    4. Believe God even before a Doctor's Confirmation

D. Understand that it's okay to seek God's Hand, Blessings, Healing, etc.

    1. A prayer for Healings, Miracles, Signs & Wonders (Acts 4:29-31)

_____

_____

_____

_____

_____

_____

_____

_____

_____

_____

_____

_____

_____

_____

_____

_____

_____

_____

2. Its God's will to bless, prosper, and heal you!

    a) Plans to prosper and bless you (Jer. 29:11-14)

    b) God want you to prosper and to be in good health (3 John 1:2).

E. Overcome the enemy

    1. A house divided can't stand (Matt. 12:22-30)

    2. First, bind the strongman (Matt. 12:29)

F. Close open doors and remove enemy inroads

    1. Repent of Doubt, Unbelief, Skepticism, and Rationalism (Luke 16:19-31)

    2. Unforgiveness (Matt. 12:22-30)

    3. Bitter Judgments (Matt. 7:1-2)

    4. Ungodly beliefs

    5. Sin/Disobedience: Go and sin no more

    6. Break word curses that you've spoken, repent, and speak words of blessings and faith, etc.

REFLECTION QUESTIONS

1. After reviewing Mark 4:14-20, what is the first way a person could lose his/her healing?

   _____

   _____

2. From Mark 4:14-20, what is the second way a person could lose his/her healing?

   _____

   _____

3. From Mark 4:14-20, what is the third way a person could lose his/her healing?

   _____

   _____

4. What are the four keys/principles for keeping your house occupied with the right Spirit?

   _____

   _____

5. Is there a specific key on which you feel you personally need to focus?

   _____

   _____

6. After reading Revelation 12:11, what are the three powerful keys you can use to keep your healing? Explain how each of them works below.

_____

_____

7. Is it okay for you to seek God's healing hand, blessings, and miracles? Explain why below.

_____

_____

8. Are there any open doors or enemy inroads in your life? If so, what are they?

_____

_____

Life Application

This lesson discussed ways to keep your healing, and the open doors and enemy inroads that keep us from walking in complete and total healing. Get alone with the Holy Spirit and your journal. Review this lesson and ask the Holy Spirit how to apply this lesson to your life. If there are any open doors or enemy inroads in your life, ask the Holy Spirit how to take care of these issues. Be sure to follow the leading of the Holy Spirit. Journal anything he shows you and anything he does in your life.

Prayer

Father God, I thank you for revealing to me through this lesson ways to walk in complete and total healing and freedom from sickness and disease. I ask that you would come fill me with Your Holy Spirit—fill every avenue and empty corner of my heart and soul. I thank you that my house is in order and that You are filling every crevice. I love You! Thank you for Your healing and miracle power resting on my life. I want to live a life of freedom and bring that freedom everywhere I go. Show me any open doors or enemy inroads into my life so that we can remove them. I bless you now in Jesus' name! Amen.

LESSON ELEVEN

hidden with Christ in God:
soaking in the secret place of power

LESSON OBJECTIVES

☛ Examine the Four Purposes of Prayer

☛ Examine Soaking Prayer

☛ Discuss the Upward Call of God

☛ Discover Ways of Entering into Rest

☛ Examine a Contemplative Prayer Model

Jesus told us to go into our prayer closets, close the door behind us, and pray to our Father in secret (Matt. 6:6). This lesson is all about drawing close to the Person of Jesus Christ through a type of listening prayer called *soaking*. Soaking prayer is the door that opens the eternal realm of heaven in our lives and releases the knowledge of the glory of the Lord in the earth. Prayer is the vehicle that connects us to heaven, keeping our old man dead and our new man alive and hidden with Christ in God. We are empowered to walk in the miraculous by living in continual fellowship with the Holy Spirit.

KEY SCRIPTURE PASSAGES

If then you have been raised with Christ [to new life, thus sharing His resurrection from the dead], **aim at and seek** *the [rich, eternal treasures]* **that are above,** *where Christ is, seated at the right hand of God. And* **set your minds and keep them set on what is above** *(the higher things), not on the things that are on the earth. For [as far as this world is concerned] you have died, and* **your [new, real] life is hidden with Christ in God** (Col. 3:1-3, AMP).

He who **dwells in the secret place** *of the Most High shall remain stable and fixed under the shadow of the Almighty* (Ps. 91:1 AMP).

Be unceasing in prayer [praying perseveringly] (1 Thess. 5:17, AMP).

I. THE FOUR PURPOSES OF PRAYER

A. Prayer Prepares

    1. Revelation of what the Father is doing (John 5:19)

    2. Revelation of Purpose

        a) Luke 4:42,43

        b) Acts 10:9-10

3. Strength for Trials (Matt. 26:35-41) _____

4. Wisdom for Decisions (Luke 6:12-13) _____

B. Prayer Empowers _____

    1. The Disciples _____

        a) Acts 1:13-14 _____

        b) Acts 2:1-4 _____

    2. Great Power (Acts 4:31-33) _____

C. Prayer Hides (often before or after
great miracles) _____

    1. Jesus' Ministry Model (John 6:2, 15) _____

    2. Jesus on the mountain (Matt. 14:23) _____

    3. In the wilderness (Luke 5:15-16) _____

    4. Long before daylight (Mark 1:34-35) _____

    5. With the Disciples (Luke 9:10) _____

D. Prayer brings death and life _____

    1. Jesus in the desert (Luke 4:1-14) _____

    2. Dying to earthly things (Col. 3:1-3) _____

    3. Dying to Sin _____

        a) Rom 6 _____

        b) Matt. 6:13 _____

_____

4. The Key to Death (John 3:28-30)

5. Crucified with Christ—alive with Him, too (Gal. 2:20)

6. Resurrected and seated with Christ at the right hand of God (Eph. 2:6)

II. WHAT DO YOU MEAN, "SOAKING"?

Soaking is a form of prayer, but not the type that probably comes to mind. Prayer in the western world often looks like a lot of rambling, a lot of asking God for something, and a lot of "religious duty." Soaking prayer has very little to do with talking to God and more to do with listening to Him. Soaking is *posturing* yourself in a place to *receive* from God after *giving* Him all of yourself. Soaking is *positioning* yourself in a place of *stillness* and *quietness*, of *meditation* and *contemplation* on the Person of Jesus Christ and the indwelling presence of the Holy Spirit. It is a place of genuine, internal *peace* and *rest*.

The reason we use the word "soaking" when referring to this type of prayer actually comes from the Greek word "baptizo," which is where we get the English word *baptize*. John the Baptist said that though he baptized in water, Jesus would baptize in the Holy Spirit and fire (Matt. 3:11. The Greek word *baptizo* means, "to dip." It actually contains all of the following meanings: *to dip repeatedly, immersing, fully submerging* (as in a sinking ship), *washing or bathing oneself,* and *overwhelming.*

We want to be soaked, fully submerged, repeatedly dipped, washed, bathed, overwhelmed, and consumed with the presence of the Holy Spirit! Like a dry and brittle sponge needs to be dipped in water, so we need to be fully submerged and baptized in the river of God's presence until every fiber of our being is filled to overflowing. In this way, we leak and spill out the glory of God everywhere we go. There are two primary Hebrew words translated into the English word "anoint" in the Old Testament; one of them means, "to rub," and the other means, "to smear." In both cases, it's talking about *rubbing* or *smearing* oil. The anointing of God is like oil: it's tangible, transferable, and, when not properly contained, has a tendency to get all over everything! Remember, it's the Person of the Holy Spirit who carries the anointing and power of God. When we spend time with Him in the presence of Jesus Christ, the Anointed One, we can't help but have the anointing of God rubbed and smeared deep into our lives and ministries. It just gets all over everything!

Jesus said that we would be baptized in the Holy Spirit (Acts 1:5), meaningwe would be soaked and completely submerged in the Holy Spirit. Soaking is like pickling. You take a cucumber and soak it in vinegar and spices, and over time it turns into a pickle! We want to go into God's presence as a cucumber and come out a juicy dill! We need to be pickled in the presence of God. Paul says in Ephesians 5:18 not to "...*get drunk with wine, for that is dissipation, but* **be filled** *with the Spirit.*" The words, "be filled," in this verse denote multiple and continual infillings of the Holy Spirit. As discussed in lesson 10, Paul is not saying that being filled with the Holy Spirit is a one time event; in the Greek it actually means, "be, being filled"; a continual infilling and submerging in the presence of God.

Many ministers and revivalists whom I know personally were released into ministry or had a major breakthrough in their ministry after a season of soaking and ministering to the Lord in the secret place. This was the case for me.

Several years ago, I entered a season of soaking and pressing hard into the Lord. I spent hours in the glory of God, lifted into His presence. Before this time, I had experienced many breakthroughs and encounters in the glory of God, but what happened next changed my life and ministry forever. I went to bed early after prayer one night because I was working and ministering to make ends meet. Often, as I went to bed, I meditated on the presence of God and extended myself into the throne room, ministering to the Lord until I fell asleep. On several occasions, the Lord entered my room and sat at the end of my bed to spend time with me. Other times, the glory of God would come over the top of my head as a lamp or a ball of light. With my eyes closed and the lights off in the bedroom, the light from the glory of God would be so intense that my whole body would shake as waves of God's love rippled over me — it was pure ecstasy!

That night, I was awakened at 11:22 pm by the blast of a trumpet. Two angels with long silver trumpets stood at the foot of my bed blowing an alarm in my ears. I felt like John must have felt on the Island of Patmos when he said he fell like a dead man. The fear of the Lord filled my body and I was completely undone in the hands of God. The angel on my left blew a trumpet in my left ear. This is what woke me up. The angel on the right blew his trumpet in my right ear. What came out wasn't sound, but a hot wind that entered my body and went into my chest, into my spirit man and exploded in electric power. Immediately, I was pulled out of my body, through the roof, through the atmosphere and the stars, and came to rest in a large room in heaven called the "Room of Intercession." I remember thinking it must be a dream. As I looked around I saw men and women, children and angels all praying over the nations. I saw regions of the earth flash before me in a moment of time. Everything was so surreal… I could scarcely take in what I saw. In the experience, I looked around and saw myself lying on the floor, yet I stood above myself at the same time. As I watched myself, praise began to flow from my spirit man. When you encounter the presence of God, what is in your heart begins to rise to the surface. I began to worship Him and say, "Lord, you're so awesome… so beautiful… Jesus, you're so wonderful and incredible…." This praise came out of my mouth, but I noticed two voices coming out of me: my voice *and* the voice of the Holy Spirit. Both voices harmoniously sang and declared the goodness of the Lord.

This encounter lasted through the evening and into the morning. As I awoke, my eyes opened to a whole new dimension in the Spirit. I prolifically saw angels, beings, and shafts of light that moved through the house like colorful supernatural pathways reaching from my living room into the heavens. My spirit man awakened to a brand new place in the glory of God. Rainbows began to appear in meetings and clouds of glory manifested as I preached. Miracles exploded in the atmosphere with tangible signs of the glory. Often, fireballs or honey wheels were released in meetings, and the whole house became whacked under the power of God. We saw gold teeth, gold dust, gemstones, and other wonderful signs with many healings and creative miracles. God shifted me, shifted the ministry, and shifted our lives: we've never been the same. God granted this encounter because I hungered and thirsted for Him with my entire being. It wouldn't have happened unless I had learned to position myself in a place of stillness, rest, and meditation on the goodness of God. Soaking is a key component in receiving breakthrough in your life and ministry. The breakthrough is the result of a heart sold out to Him!

III. THE UPWARD CALL AND TABERNACLING WITH GOD

[For my determined purpose is] that I may know Him [that I may progressively become more deeply and intimately acquainted with Him, perceiving and recognizing and understanding the wonders of His Person more strongly and more clearly].... **I press on toward the goal** *to win the [supreme and heavenly] prize to which God in Christ Jesus is* **calling us upward** (Phil. 3:10, 14, AMP).

The whole purpose of soaking, and the entirety of Christianity for that matter, is to walk in a love relationship with Jesus Christ: getting to know Him, His character and nature. Throughout Paul's epistles we see a golden thread—a unique strand—that tied together all of his writings. This golden thread is the upward call of God in Christ Jesus (Phil. 3:14): it is being heavenly minded, setting our minds, hearts, and affections on things above where Christ is seated and where we are seated with Him in the heavenly realm (Eph. 2:6; Col. 3:1-3). The author of Hebrews tells us to boldly come before the throne of grace, which exists in heaven (Heb. 4:16), and to set our gaze firmly on Jesus Christ, the risen and ruling King (Heb. 12:2).

> *He [God] also has planted eternity in men's hearts and minds* (Eccl. 3:11, AMP, emphasis added).

Both Isaiah and Ezekiel had incredible throne room encounters (Isa. 6:1-13; Ez. 1:26-28). What they saw was beautiful and amazing, yet their understanding and perception was *in part* because they didn't know Christ. John the Revelator was a man like us—a born again, Spirit filled believer. Something about heaven and the realm of eternity seized his being. When banished to the Island of Patmos, John was given a great opportunity to get to know the resurrected Christ more. I can see him praying, pressing in, and worshiping God *in the Spirit* (Rev. 1:10). Undoubtedly, he had read of Isaiah and Ezekiel's throne room encounters and was longing for his own. The next thing you know, he hears a trumpet, and a voice, and is sucked up into the heavenlies to have one of the most amazing encounters ever recorded! Isaiah and Ezekiel saw dimly the throne and the One who sat on the throne. John saw the same thing, but received a greater unfolding of the revelation of the glory of the Lord. Likewise, when we encounter God on His throne, He can reveal different aspects, characteristics, and revelations of His Person and glory.

Paul had a similar experience:

> *Boasting is necessary, though it is not profitable; but I will go on to visions and revelations of the Lord. I know a man in Christ who fourteen years ago—whether in the body I do not know, or out of the body I do not know, God knows—such a man was caught up to the third heaven. And I know how such a man... was caught up into Paradise and heard inexpressible words, which a man is not permitted to speak. On behalf of such a man I will boast; but on my own behalf I will not boast, except in regard to my weaknesses (2 Cor. 12:1-6).*

Paul and John were both caught up and saw the throne in paradise in the third heaven. John was able to write down the experience, which became the book of Revelation. Paul, on the other hand, was only permitted to speak of the experience to a degree—it seems for the purpose of staying humble (vs 6-10). Paul and John's ministries and callings were different. John was not only permitted to share what he saw, but was also commanded to write it down. Paul's calling was different; he was heavily involved with the body of Christ and church politics, growth, do's and don'ts, etc. Even though Paul wasn't permitted to publically share his experience, the revelations from his third heaven encounter obviously leaked out through his life and in all of his ministry and writings.

Our aim is to know God as intimately as He can be known. The only thing that will quench the thirst for eternity in our hearts is our response to the invitation to go up the mountain of the Lord to meet with Him. We must individually and corporately behold the Lord in all of His glory! When we do this, when we are lifted into His presence, His presence comes down. When we spend time in heaven, heaven comes to earth. When our praises go up, His glory comes down. The more time we spend wrapped in the secret place, the more we will drip heaven's presence everywhere we walk on the earth. We become a conduit—a glory dispenser! When we go up and make our home with Him, He comes down and makes His home with us. I want God to make His home with me! I want Him to dwell, settle down, rest, and abide on my life! I want Him to tabernacle with me—I want to be His tabernacle!

> *Jesus answered, "If a person [really] loves Me, he will keep My word [obey My teaching]; and My Father will love him, and We will come to him and make Our home (abode, special dwelling place) with him"* (John 14:23, AMP).

God has always wanted to make His tabernacle in the earth. This was His original intention in the Garden of Eden and this will be the grand finale in Revelation 21:3, *"Behold, the tabernacle of God is among men, and He will dwell among them, and they shall be His people, and God Himself will be among them."*

IV. BE STILL AND KNOW—ENTERING INTO REST

Psalm 46:10 says, *"Be still, and know that I am God,"* (NIV). The word "still" means *idle, quiet,* and *alone.* In this verse, the word "know" takes several phrases to explain the full meaning: *come to know by experience, perceive, find, see, be made known, become known, be revealed,* and *cause to know.* The psalmist, David, was the master of the *Selah.* That word signifies *rest.* It means *to pause and calmly think and meditate in a place of rest and peace.* I can see David journaling psalm after psalm and worshiping God. Then he takes a *Selah*—he pauses and meditates. When he got more revelation he would begin writing again; when finished, he would pause and take another *Selah* until he got more revelation. I think he used it as a means of *divine listening.* In the same way, I came to a level of understanding of the Person of God that brought breakthrough in my ministry—all coming from practicing *Selah,* or divine listening.

> *For the one who has entered His rest has himself also rested from works, as God did from His. Therefore let us be diligent to enter that rest, so that no one will fall, through following the same example of disobedience…. And to whom did He swear that they would not enter His rest, but to those who were disobedient? So we see that they were not able to enter because of unbelief* (Heb. 4:10-11; 3:18-19).

V. PARTAKING OF HIS DIVINE NATURE —BEHOLDING AND BECOMING

A. Partaking of His Divine Nature

1. *...by which have been given to us exceedingly great and precious promises, that through these you may be partakers of the divine nature...* (2 Peter 1:4).

2. *...Jesus said to them, "I am the bread of life; he who comes to Me will not hunger, and he who believes in Me will never thirst* (John 6:35).

B. Beholding and Becoming—Seeing the Face of God

1. *...but whenever a person turns to the Lord, the veil is taken away. Now the Lord is the Spirit, and where the Spirit of the Lord is, there is liberty. But we all, with unveiled face, beholding as in a mirror the glory of the Lord, are being transformed into the same image from glory to glory, just as from the Lord, the Spirit* (2 Cor. 3:16-18).

2. *For God Who said, Let light shine out of darkness, has shone in our hearts so as [to beam forth] the Light for the illumination of the knowledge of the majesty and glory of God [as it is manifest in the Person and is revealed] in the face of Jesus Christ (the Messiah)* (2 Cor. 4:6, AMP).

VI. THE GREATEST COMMANDMENT AND THE RESULT OF IT!

"Teacher, which is the great commandment in the Law?" And He said to him, "'You shall love the Lord your God with all your heart, and with all your soul, and with all your mind.' This is the great and foremost commandment. The second is like it, 'You shall love your neighbor as yourself.' On these two commandments depend the whole Law and the Prophets' " (Matt. 22:36-40).

There was a corporate prophetic word released some-time in the 90s that was used to shift church back into intimacy with the Lord. The word from the Lord was, "Seek My face, not my hand." What we must understand is that prophetic words are "now" words; they aren't meant to build theology, doctrine, or tradition around. Prophetic words release the heart of God during that season at that specific time. This was a much-needed word during that season because many people were pursuing the hand of God (His works) without seeking His face (intimacy and relationship). That was the word of the Lord *then*, but not *now*! And the prophetic word of the Lord *today* will not be the prophetic word of the Lord *tomorrow*! Does that make sense? Many people have taken that word and built theology around it—they say we aren't allowed to seek the hand of God: the miracles, healings, gifts, anointings, etc. This is wrong. The Bible clearly instructs us to pursue His gifts, *"...earnestly desire and cultivate the spiritual endowments (gifts), especially that you may prophesy.... But earnestly desire and zeal-ously cultivate the greatest and best gifts and graces (the higher gifts and the choicest graces)* (1 Cor. 14:1; 12:31, AMP). So, I'm trying to drive this home—we need to seek both the *face* of God and the *hand* of God.

With that being said, the face of God and intimacy with Him should be of utmost concern and our greatest endeavor. It's perfectly fine to go into an intense season of seeking the gifts and greater anointing and breakthrough so that the power of God can flow through you to transform other people's lives. But if you find this is all your heart longs for, and you're not cultivating your relationship with Him other than for this purpose, it's time to confess and repent. That's a dangerous place to be!

> *Many will say to Me on that day, "Lord, Lord, did we not prophesy in Your name, and in Your name cast out demons, and in Your name perform many miracles?" And then I will declare to them, "I never knew you; depart from Me, you who practice lawlessness"* (Matt. 7:21-23).

Many people put so much of a priority on ministering to others that they forget true ministry is *an overflow of their relationship with God.* We have a bunch of dry Christians performing their religious duties, which carries no eternal value or weight because it's not out of intimacy with the Holy Spirit. These people may even have the right intentions of wanting to help others! But Jesus said, *"...apart from Me you can do nothing."* Jesus is saying that apart from abiding in the Vine we can do nothing that has any *eternal weight* or *value*; it may look good in the moment, but it will be burnt up in fire because it's just wood, hay, and stubble:

> *Now if any man builds on the foundation with gold, silver, precious stones, wood, hay, straw, each man's work will become evident; for the day will show it because it is to be revealed with fire, and the fire itself will test the quality of each man's work* (1 Cor. 3:12-13).

The greatest commandment is to love God with everything in us. The second greatest is to love people as ourselves. We need to make sure we get this straight. If serving people and ministering to them is more of a priority than walking in relationship and obedience to God, we're getting the commands confused. We first need to be sold out to God: that is, taking up our cross and following Him. This means practicing purity of heart, mind, and body, and walking in obedience. When we make His face our goal, we will be so filled and flooded with the life, power, and anointing of God that we can't help but love people to wholeness and see their lives transformed.

When we spend time in the secret place, God rewards us openly (Matt. 6:6, NKJV). Nothing can compare with the benefits, results, and outcomes of being intimate with Jesus. As we begin to hear and discern His voice clearly he gives us supernatural wisdom and revelation. We are commissioned into our calling, we receive mantles, and increase in our anointing. As we behold His image, we take on His character and nature. We really become the body of Christ. We are His hands and feet. We are Jesus in the earth. Like the Lord said in Exodus 7:1 concerning Moses, *we become as God to*

Pharaoh (the world).

VII. SIX INGREDIENTS OF THE CONTEMPLATIVE STATE

A. Physical Calm

1. Heb. 4:9-11

2. Heb. 3:18-19

B. Focused Attention

1. Heb. 12:1-2

2. John 5:19

C. Letting Be

1. Ps. 46:10

2. Phil. 4:6-7

D. Receptivity (John 15:4-5)

E. Spontaneous Flow (John 7:38-39)

F. Beholding (2 Cor. 3:18)

VIII. A CONTEMPLATIVE PRAYER MODEL

A. Letting Go of everything but the here and now

Begin by laying aside your past, all of your victories and defeats. Lay down your future, your desires, and concerns. It meditate on God in the *here and now*, casting all our anxieties on Him for He cares for us. All of the Kingdom of heaven resides in your spirit man. It's okay to turn inward, to sink inside in order to hear the voice of God. You can use your imagination to picture the cloud of God's presence wrapping around you. This isn't new age. The imagination was given to you by God and is a tool to engage heaven. Jesus taught in parables and engaged people's imaginations in order to lead them into a deeper walk with God.

B. Prayer of Quiet

At the center of our being we are hushed. We have entered into a listening stillness. All the outward and inward distractions have been silenced and our spirit is completely engaged and on alert to hear and experience God. We bask in the warmth of His presence and focus on Him!

C. Ecstasy

The Greek word is *ekstasis*, which is most often translated into the English word, "trance." This state of being is granted by the Lord Himself and cannot be achieved by our own efforts. It is a state of being completely unaware of our surroundings and completely caught up with the Lord.

D. Becoming completely still and beholding Him in all of His glory

Coming to a place of total stillness during prayer is a great challenge. If we are going to commune with God, first we must become still. Habakkuk went to his guard post to pray (Hab. 2:1). In the early morning when it was still dark, Jesus departed to a lonely place to pray (Mark 1:35). After an entire day filled with ministry, Jesus went to a mountain to pray. Stillness is not necessarily the goal: it's a means to go deeper with God. It is the door in which we are able to fellowship and commune with the Lord spirit to Spirit. Coming to a place of total stillness cannot be hurried, forced, or accomplished because of your ability or self-effort. Rather, it must be allowed to happen. At a point in your stillness, God begins to take over and you sense His active flow within you. At this point, spontaneous images begin to flow with a life of their own. He speaks, and you hear. He imparts supernatural strength, wisdom, and endowments in this place of stillness.

IX. DEALING WITH DISTRACTIONS

A. Outward Distractions

There are many outward distractions that can pull you away from pressing into God. If you're at your house, it could be the phone, neighbors, pets, kids, chores and cleaning, unwanted guests, email, texting, television, etc. At first, when prac-

_____

_____

_____

_____

_____

_____

_____

_____

_____

_____

_____

_____

_____

_____

_____

_____

_____

_____

_____

ticing the presence of God, it may be necessary to eliminate outward distractions as much as possible. It's also helpful to set aside time every day— normally the same time every day—to pray, meditate, and practice soaking. This helps develop a pattern and a discipline for feasting on God's presence. Later, after doing this for a while, you will actually learn to carry the same presence of God that you experience during your soaking sessions into the work place, school, grocery shopping, etc. You become a barer of His glory and power when you learn to stay in the secret place while doing everyday tasks. This happens through continual worship, prayer, adoration, and beholding Him.

B. Inward Distractions

For most people, inward distractions are a little more difficult to take care of than the outward type. When you're pressing in, and all you can think about is your "To do" list, I've found it helpful to take a minute to write down all the things you have to do. This helps remove it from your mind and subconscious because you know you can refer back to that list later. If you feel a block because of some type of sin, or if you're very sin-conscience, confess it, repent, get rid of it, and keep moving forward. It's been nailed to the cross. If you've confessed and God has forgiven you, you must also forgive yourself. If you find that your mind wanders aimlessly, it's helpful to speak in tongues, sing and worship, focus on Jesus, and/or meditate on the Word until your mind becomes still.

REFLECTION QUESTIONS

1. What are the four purposes of prayer?

_____

_____

2. What is soaking? Describe it in your own words.

_____

_____

3. In the Hebrew, what are the two meanings for the word anoint?

_____

_____

4. What does the Bible mean when it talks about God making His tabernacle on the earth?

_____

_____

5. What are some ways we enter into the rest of God?

_____

_____

6. What is the greatest commandment? Describe what it looks like to walk out the commandment in your life.

_____

_____

7. What are five ingredients for the contemplative state?

    _____

    _____

8. What are the points described in the contemplative prayer model in this lesson?

    _____

    _____

Activity and Questions for Group Discussion

1. In a group setting, put on some light worship or instrumental music. Find a comfortable place to sit or lie down. Spend a set amount of time soaking (10 to 30 minutes). Invite the Holy Spirit to come, and meditate on His indwelling presence.

2. Get back together and take turns discussing what happened. Did you see or hear anything? Did you feel or sense the presence of the Lord? What were some hindrances or distractions to pressing in? What did the Lord do? Do you feel empowered by the Holy Spirit in any way? Have fun with the discussion and learn from each other's encounters.

Life Application

Grab your journal or notebook and get alone with God. Quiet yourself and still your mind before the Lord (Ps. 46:10). If you haven't had much experience doing this, it will take some practice at first. That's right! It actually takes practice and spiritual exercise to learn how to discern the voice of the Holy Spirit. Turning off all the mental noises, thoughts, and concerns is easier said than done. However, you're not necessarily trying to turn them off and become void, as many New Agers teach when giving instruction on meditation.

We don't want to be void of anything—we want to be filled with Jesus so He takes over our thoughts, imaginations, desires, etc. As believers, we don't meditate on nothing; He is our point of focus. Oftentimes, when engaging the presence of the Lord, we actually have to sink into ourselves. We're not trying to hear a voice that thunders from heaven—an impersonal force that exists somewhere in the expanse. We are listening for the still small voice that whispers from within. All the treasures of wisdom and knowledge are hidden in the Person of Jesus Christ (Col. 2:3); this same Jesus lives in your heart (Eph. 3:17), and your spirit has been made one spirit with the Holy Spirit (1 Cor. 6:17). Open yourself to hear from the Holy Spirit and be led by Him. Journal anything you receive or any experience that takes place.

Prayer

Father God, I ask that You would give me a revelation of Christ in me the hope of glory—a revelation of the Kingdom within, the anointing within, and God's seed growing in my spirit man. Teach me how to live and walk in your Kingdom, and let creative miracles begin to pop open in my life. I thank You for Your saving, healing, and miracle power on my life. I ask that You would give me opportunities to walk in your creative power. Increase my faith so that I see a release and demonstration of Kingdom power and glory. I worship You, praise You, and give You all the glory to, in Jesus' precious name, Amen!

LESSON TWELVE
the word of knowledge

LESSON OBJECTIVES

- ☛ Examine briefly the nine gifts of the Holy Spirit
- ☛ Discuss how to operate in the word of knowledge
- ☛ Discover how the word of knowledge is used with other gifts of the Spirit
- ☛ Examine Old and New Testament examples of the word of knowledge
- ☛ Discover ways you can receive words of knowledge
- ☛ Examine Old and New Testament examples of the word of knowledge
- ☛ Discuss when, where, and how to give a word of knowledge

The gift of the word of knowledge is one of the nine gifts of the Holy Spirit. Receiving a word of knowledge is receiving information by supernatural means regarding a person or group of people that you previously did not know by natural means. This powerful gift complements the healing and miracle gifts dramatically. A word of knowledge sparks faith in the hearer, allowing them to access their healing or miracle. In this lesson, we'll discuss how to operate in the word of knowledge and how it can be used with other gifts of the Spirit. We'll look at Old and New Testament examples of the word of knowledge, and we'll discover ways you can receive words of knowledge. Finally, we'll examine when, where, and how to give a word of knowledge.

KEY SCRIPTURE PASSAGE

*But to each one is given the manifestation of the [Holy] Spirit [the evidence, the spiritual illumination of the Spirit] for good and profit. To one is given in and through the [Holy] Spirit [the power to speak] a **message of wisdom**, and to another [the power to express] a **word of knowledge** and understanding according to the same [Holy] Spirit; to another [wonder-working] **faith** by the same [Holy] Spirit, to another the **extraordinary powers of healing** by the one Spirit; to another the **working of miracles**, to another **prophetic insight** (the gift of interpreting the divine will and purpose); to another the **ability to discern and distinguish between** [utterances of true] **spirits** [and false ones], to another various kinds of [unknown] **tongues**, to another the ability to interpret [such] **tongues** (1 Cor. 12:7-10, AMP).*

I. BRIEF DEFINITIONS OF THE NINE GIFTS OF THE HOLY SPIRIT

*But to each one is given the manifestation of the Spirit for the common good. For to one is given the **word of wisdom** through the Spirit, and to another the **word of knowledge** according to the same Spirit; to another **faith** by the same Spirit, and to another **gifts of healing** by the one Spirit, and to another the* *effecting of miracles, and to another prophecy, and to another the distinguishing of spirits, to another various kinds of tongues, and to another the interpretation of tongues* (1 Cor.12:7-10).

A. Utterance Gifts: Speaking, Worship, Prayer, Inspiration, Bubbling Up

1. The Gift of Tongues

A gift that allows you to speak in the tongue of men or angels (unknown to the speaker at the exact time of delivery), which is used for personal prayer, praising God, and stirring up your spirit man. When interpreted, the gift of tongues is used for corporate exhortation.

2. The Gift of Interpretation of Tongues

The ability to interpret the utterance of tongues for corporate exhortation. If you have this gift, you can interpret your tongue and other people's tongues.

3. The Gift of Prophecy

The ability to speak, decree, or deliver a message from the Lord, speaking the mind, heart, and will of God—acting as His mouthpiece. The gift of prophecy is for encouraging, exhorting, and comforting the body of Christ. The gift of prophecy deals with future events of what God desires to do, or with circumstances the Lord wants us to pray about in order to bring a different outcome. The gift of prophecy is foresight of the future, which is used for delivering a timely message bringing direction.

B. Revelation Gifts: Information, Instruction, Direction, Discernment

1. The Gift of the Word of Knowledge

A word of knowledge usually is information concerning the present or the past, whereas prophecy is concerning future events. Words of knowledge are information received by supernatural means regarding a person or group of people that you previously did not know by natural means.

2. The Gift of the Word of Wisdom

Wisdom is simply understanding how to apply revelation. The gift of the word of wisdom is understanding what to do with a word of knowledge when you get one.

3. The Gift of Discerning of Spirits

The gift of discerning of spirits is the supernatural ability to perceive the presence (or non-presence) of a demonic spirit, angelic beings, the Holy Spirit, and thoughts and attitudes of the heart and mind.

C. Power Gifts: Action, Evangelism, Demonstration

    1. The Gift of Wonder-working Faith

    The gift of faith is a firm supernatural conviction and belief in Jesus Christ to accomplish the impossible—healings, miracles, signs, wonders, financial provision, etc.—by your spoken word, according to God's promises in His Word, or expressed through a word of knowledge, word of wisdom, or discerning of spirits.

    2. The Gift of Miracles

    The gift for the working of miracles causes supernatural phenomena that supersede natural laws and explanations to take place, in the name of Jesus.

    3. The Gifts of Healing

    The gifts of healing bring a supernatural cure, restoration, and/or wholeness to a person's physical body. This could be instantt or over a certain period of time. Healings are an extension of God's miracle power. Notice the word "gifts" is plural. There are lots of different types of healing gifts. You can have a gift of healing for knees, headaches, blind eyes, etc.

_____

_____

_____

_____

_____

_____

_____

_____

_____

_____

_____

_____

_____

_____

_____

_____

_____

_____

_____

_____

II. OPERATING IN THE WORD OF KNOWLEDGE

A. A Deeper Look

John Wimber, one of the founding leaders of the Vineyard Movement, defined Word of knowledge as supernatural revelation of a fact about a person or situation, which is not learned through the efforts of the natural mind, but is a fragment of knowledge freely given by God, disclosing the truth which the Spirit wishes to be made known concerning a particular person or situation.

The Apostle Paul received lots of words of knowledge: *"Now we have received, not the spirit of the world, but the Spirit who is from God, so that we may know the things freely given to us by God, which things we also speak, not in words taught by human wisdom, but in those taught by the Spirit, combining spiritual thoughts with spiritual words* (1 Cor. 2:12-13).

B. Word of Knowledge used with other gifts

For example: in a meeting you may receive a word of knowledge for someone by the name of Rachel who is 21 and who needs healing in her foot. She stands and you then you get a word of wisdom for her to step out into the isle and by faith reach down and touch her toes. When she does, Rachel receives her healing. Then you prophesy how, just as the enemy would try to take out her "foot," it's also been an attack on her "walk" and relationship with God and today is a fresh day to start walking with Him in a new grace and favor. When flowing in the Holy Spirit sometimes the lines between gifts are blurred!

III. THE WORD OF KNOWLEDGE IN THE OLD TESTAMENT

A. 16 Words of Knowledge! King's Anointing Confirmed (1 Sam. 10:1-16)

B. A Warning for a King (2 Kings 6:8-10)

C. Instructions for the Ark's Construction (Gen. 6:14-22)

D. Unveiling of a Lie (2 Kings 5:20-27)

E. Knowledge of a Successor (1 Kings 19:15-16)

IV. THE WORD OF KNOWLEDGE IN THE NEW TESTAMENT

A. An Incredible Soul-Winning Tool (John 4:4-42)

B. For Provision (Matt. 17:27)

C. Warning of danger (Acts 22:17-21)

D. Divine knowledge of direction (Acts 9:10-16)

E. Revelation of sin (Acts 5:1-5)

V. PREPARATION FOR MOVING IN THE WORD OF KNOWLEDGE

_____
_____
_____
_____
_____
_____
_____
_____
_____
_____
_____
_____
_____
_____
_____
_____
_____
_____
_____

A. Clean Heart

    1. Ps. 66:18

    2. 1 John 1:9

B. Earnestly desire to move in word of knowledge. You can ask, seek, pursue, and earnestly desire the gifts of the Spirit (1 Cor. 14:1). We're even told to "…*earnestly desire and zealously cultivate the greatest and best gifts*" (1 Cor. 12:31, AMP). Many people think it's wrong to desire spiritual gifts—the Bible shouts otherwise! I've heard it taught that desiring spiritual gifts is selfish, prideful, etc. Remember, gifts of the Holy Spirit aren't for your benefit; they're given for the purpose of advancing the Kingdom of God in the lives of men, women, and children around you. Think about it!

C. Be willing to step out when you actually get a word of knowledge! Jesus said, "*Freely you received, freely give*" (Matt. 10:8). If you want more for yourself, and to continually increase in word of knowledge for healing, you have to be ready to do the stuff.

VI. A FEW WAYS TO RECEIVE A WORD OF KNOWLEDGE

God speaks to His people in countless ways. He can give us a word of knowledge any way He wants. Below are some of the more common ways we can receive words of knowledge from the Spirit of God for healing.

A. External Impression
(Feeling in your physical body)

You may get a sharp, dull, or throbbing sensation in part of your body. These can vary, being minor, or sometimes quite intense. If you're not sure whether or not it's from God, simply dialogue with Him and ask. You can ask Him if the sensation is a word of knowledge and for Him to take it away. If it's Him, generally it will go away unless He's trying to communicate something else. Sometimes you my experience a strong emotion such as anxiety, fear, or panic. This would likely be a word of knowledge for some type of demonic oppression.

Use discernment, and make sure this isn't a normal condition in your own body. If you normally have pain in your knees, it's probably your knees and not a word of knowledge. A good thing to do is consciously check your body in the morning for any type of pain, irritation, etc. Then throughout your day if you feel something, it's likely a word for someone around you.

B. Internal Impression (Simple thought or internal sense or prompting)

This would enter into your mind as a simple thought, sense, or prompting. It could be explained as simple intuition: you know that you know that you know, but you're not sure how you know. These promptings bubble up from your spirit-man (where the Holy Spirit dwells), and once they enter your mind, you become aware of them to process.

C. Speaking

This is similar to the type of prophet that has prophetic words just bubble forth from his spirit man. This can happen while talking, praying, prophesying, or standing with someone — unpremeditated words roll out of your mouth concerning a physical condition that you weren't previously aware of.

D. The Seer Realm (Dream, Vision, Quick Mental Picture, Reading a Word).

1. Mental Picture

In your mind's eye you may see a picture of an arm, lung, head, etc.; someone with a physical condition such as a cast, crutches, or a limp, etc.; or even an accident like a car crash or someone tripping over railroad tracks, etc.

2. Dream or Vision

You may have a dream or vision of you or someone with a health problem. This often is a word of knowledge for healing — or even a specific gift of healing being released for this particular condition. In the dream or vision, you could simply hear someone talking about a health problem or a messenger (angel) could come to you in order to give you information.

3. Reading a Word

In your mind, you could see a word written over a person, on his/her forehead, or really anywhere. This could be displayed as a banner or newspaper headline.

4. A Revelatory Experience (Trance and Visionary Encounter)

Similar to a dream, you could have a lifelike 3D type experience or encounter that feels like you're actually there. Often these types of visionary experiences are released while a person is in a trance-like state.

E. Miscellaneous

   1. Still Small Voice

   2. Inner Audible

   3. Audible

   4. Circumstance

   5. Road Sign

   6. Nature

   7. Numbers

   8. Any other way God wants to speak to you

VII.TIMING OF WORDS OF KNOWLEDGE

Words of knowledge can come at any time: during a prayer meeting, home group, church service, supermarket, on the job, brushing your teeth, or on your bed at night. You may or may not know whom the word is for. Oftentimes the word is for someone who is present; however, it may be for a person someone present knows or someone you see in a day or two.

VIII. WHEN AND HOW TO GIVE A WORD OF KNOWLEDGE

First of all, when you receive a word of knowledge for a specific person, it's good to ask yourself if this is a word that you should give to someone, or if it's something to be prayed about. Because we are the Lord's friends, He'll sometimes show us something about someone so we can pray for them and not simply say, "The Lord showed me this about you."

It's good, at first, to be tentative about speaking a word of knowledge. Instead of saying, "The Lord just told me there is someone here who has back pain," it might be better to ask, "Is there anyone here with back pain?" If there is, great! Ask them if you can pray for their back to be healed! If there's not, then it's not that big of a deal… you might have missed it, or maybe the word is actually for somebody in the next room or someone you're going to meet in 30 minutes. If a person wants prayer later, then pray for them later. If the person is too embarrassed to receive prayer, you can give loving encouragement… don't condemn or overreact and get upset. If the person still refuses, there's no need to pressure him/her anymore.

If you receive a word of knowledge during a large meeting, it's best not to say anything unless the leader provides an opportunity for words to be given. You could also ask an usher or someone in authority if they know the protocol for giving words at that particular church or fellowship. Always keep your eyes open, both in the natural and in the spirit, for someone to cross your path who may have the condition God revealed to you.

The more details you have when giving a word, the more faith you'll spark in the person it's for. If you're in a meeting with 100 people, and you give a word in front of everybody about knee pain, it's likely there are five or more people with knee pain. If you get a word for knee pain, ask the Lord for more details: "Male or female? What age group? First or middle name?" If the Lord shows you anything, great! If not, don't worry about giving the simple word about knee pain. Who knows? Maybe everybody's knees will be healed!

IX. HEALING EVANGELISM WITH WORDS OF KNOWLEDGE

Just as the Father sent Jesus into the world we are being sent! The message of the Kingdom gospel, with demonstrations of Kingdom power, was never meant to be restricted to the boundaries of the four walls of a church building. We, as the church, have a mandate to take God's saving and healing power to the marketplace, during work, and on the streets! One of the ways this is accomplished is through words of knowledge for healing. It's hard for somebody to deny that Jesus Christ is alive and is God when their deaf ear pops open, their leg grows out, or metal dissolves in their body!

REFLECTION QUESTIONS

1.   What are the nine gifts of the Holy Spirit?

     _____

     _____

2.   In your own words, what exactly is a word of knowledge?

     _____

     _____

3.   The word of knowledge commonly works with what three other gifts of the Holy Spirit?

     _____

     _____

4.   Give an Old and New Testament example of a word of knowledge.

     _____

     _____

5.   What are the three preparations listed in this lesson for moving in the word of knowledge?

     _____

     _____

6.   List below five ways the Holy Spirit can give you a word of knowledge.

     _____

     _____

7. When do words of knowledge come? How do you know whom the word is for?

_____

_____

8. Explain below how you would give a word of knowledge while visiting a church you've never attended.

_____

_____

Questions for Group Discussion

1. In a small group setting, take turns sharing about times you've received words of knowledge. If you've never received a word of knowledge that's okay—you're about to!

2. What are some things you feel the Holy Spirit prompting you to do now that you've been through this lesson? How could you increase the word of knowledge gift in your life? Take turns sharing.

Life Application

Like I mentioned earlier, Jesus wants to take His words of knowledge and healing power to the streets. Get in a small group or with a partner… it's time for a treasure hunt! Ask the Lord where he would have you go or to give you words of knowledge for somebody. Open yourself up to hear. After taking about 10 to 20 minutes, get back with your group or partner and compare notes. Oftentimes each person gets a piece of the puzzle. Now, hit the streets and follow the leading of the Holy Spirit! Make sure you stay with your partner or group and stay in safe places—of course, the safest places are the places the Holy Spirit is leading you!

Prayer

Father God, right now I thank you for the release and activation of the gift of word of knowledge. Like Paul exhorted us to earnestly seek and desire spiritual gifts, I ask right now for a release of revelatory gifts especially for words of knowledge. I open myself up right now to you Holy Spirit to move and flow in this gift and receive specific, detailed, and accurate words daily for those who cross my path. Give me the wisdom and discernment on how and when to share the word—to encourage, uplift, and sow seeds of your love into those around me. I ask that with the word of knowledge you would also release manifestations and demonstrations of your power with healings and miracles in Jesus' name. Amen.

LESSON THIRTEEN
resurrection power

LESSON OBJECTIVES

☛ Discuss the coming resurrection revival

☛ Examine the Person of Jesus Christ as the Resurrection and the Life

☛ Discover the realm of endless possibilities in the Kingdom

☛ Discover the keys to unlock resurrection power in your life

As born again, Spirit-filled sons and daughters of God, we have a mandate to raise the dead! Death creeps into many places: physical bodies, spiritual lives, personal finances, businesses, churches, etc. Jesus said in John 10:10 that the enemy comes to steal, kill, and destroy, but He came to give us abundant life! We are called to raise those who are spiritually dead and even physically dead—to raise up dead businesses, dried up finances, and even cities overtaken with death! In this lesson, we will talk about the coming resurrection revival, examine the Person of Jesus Christ as the Resurrection and the Life, discover the realm of endless possibilities in the Kingdom, and finally, talk about keys that will unlock resurrection power into your life!

KEY SCRIPTURE PASSAGES

Jesus said to her, "I am the resurrection and the life; he who believes in Me will live even if he dies, and everyone who lives and believes in Me will never die. Do you believe this?" (John 11:25-26).

For if the dead are not raised, not even Christ has been raised; and if Christ has not been raised, your faith is worthless; you are still in your sins (1 Cor. 15:16-17).

But if the Spirit of Him who raised Jesus from the dead dwells in you, He who raised Christ Jesus from the dead will also give life to your mortal bodies through His Spirit who dwells in you (Rom. 8:11).

And as you go, preach, saying, "The kingdom of heaven is at hand. Heal the sick, raise the dead, cleanse the lepers, cast out demons. Freely you received, freely give" (Matt. 10:7-8).

I. RESURRECTION REVIVAL

I believe there is a coming Resurrection Revival! This revival will cause those places where death has ruled to be overcome and swallowed up by the life of Christ and His resurrection power. This revival will cause those who have lost vision and hope to be revitalized. Businesses touched by the sting of death will be revived by the living breath of God. Places where finances have dried up will be overtaken by the river of God's provision and blessing. This revival will not only be marked by a spiritual awakening, but by the resurrection of those who have died physically! It's going to be glorious! This is what we're pressing into!

II. JESUS IS THE RESURRECTION

    A. Seeing through Christ's Eyes (John 11:1-15)

    B. The Resurrection and the Life (John 11:25)

III. ENDLESS POSSIBILITIES!

    A. With God all things are possible (Matt. 19:26)

    B. God makes dead ends into highways of acceleration (Isa. 35:3-8)

    C. Death is an opportunity for life (John 11:15)

    D. Mountains into plains (Zech. 4:7)

IV. A CAUTION WHEN RAISING THE DEAD

Raising the dead isn't exactly like moving in healing or miracles. It's important to be sensitive to the dead person's family and friends. There have been some who wanted to raise the dead, but have done so in such an aggressive way that they deeply offended the dead person's family and friends, and moved past their wishes and desires. There's a difference between having the family and friends ask for prayer for resurrection, and just barging into a morgue demanding to pray for the dead. This can cause several issues. Jesus waited until the family and friends of Lazarus came to Him out of need. We need to either be invited to pray for the dead or hear the clear word of the Lord to move forward in faith. It's not something we do out of desire, ambition, and zeal while paying no attention to the deceased person's family and friends.

V. UNLOCKING RESURRECTION POWER IN YOUR LIFE

A. Faith lays hold of the promise now (Mark 11:24).

B. Understand that God is never early and never late (Mark 5:21-24, 35-42)

C. Contend for Your Inheritance

1. Thanksgiving and Praise—Giving Glory to God (Rom. 4:20)

2. Get excited when things are dark; you are on the verge of breakthrough (John 11:15)

D. Only Believe (Mark 5:36)

E. Focus on the three things that remain
(1 Cor. 13:13)

F. Moving in Abraham's faith and not giving into
unbelief gives you access to the life of God—He
gives life to the dead and calls into being that
which does not exist (Rom. 4:17-20)

G. Your miracle begins in your spirit! You need
to see your miracle in your spirit before it will
manifest. As you meditate, focus, and put faith in
the unseen, it will be birthed and manifested in
the natural. The life of God and all of heaven's
resources flow from your spirit
(Heb. 11:1)

H. It's sometimes necessary to war and contend
for miracles and the promises of God until they
manifest.

   1. Believe and seek (Heb. 11:6)

   2. The Shunammite Woman and Son
(2 Kings 4:8-37)

REFLECTION QUESTIONS

1. What do you believe about the coming Resurrection Revival?

_____

_____

2. Who is the Person of Resurrection in Scripture? Cite Scripture verses below.

_____

_____

3. Why are there endless possibilities as a believer?

_____

_____

4. Why is there a caution when raising the physically dead? Explain below.

_____

_____

5. Faith lays hold of the promise now. What does this mean?

_____

_____

6. How do you contend for your inheritance?

_____

_____

7. What are the three things that remain? Why should we seek to move in them now?

_____

_____

8. What does it mean when we talk about your miracle beginning in your spirit? Explain below.

_____

_____

Questions for Group Discussion

1. Discuss all your views concerning the coming resurrection revival. What does it look like? What differences are there compared to past revivals? What can we do to help bring this revival into the now?

2. Talk about what it means for your miracle to begin in your spirit. How does meditation on the promise bring it to pass? What are some places in your life that you want the Lord to bring to life with His resurrection power?

Life Application

Write below some areas of your life you want the Lord to touch with His resurrection power. This can include family and friends as well.

_____

_____

_____

Ask the Holy Spirit how to pray and how to bring these promises to pass. Write what He speaks to you below:

_____

_____

_____

_____

Prayer

Holy Spirit, I position myself before You and ask that you would release the resurrection power and life of Christ Jesus into every area of my life. Touch my heart, touch my finances, touch my future. I choose now to align myself with Your Word and Your promises concerning my life. Bring to life all the dead places. Cause me to come alive 100% and to move in Your resurrection power and Your love. Thank you for the lives that will be touched and transformed through your breath of life! In Jesus' name, Amen!

LESSON FOURTEEN
authority over the demonic

LESSON OBJECTIVES

- Examine the roles of Demonic Spirits
- Discover the "open doors" through which demonic spirits operate
- Discuss some methods of freedom from the demonic

Oftentimes, while ministering healing and moving in miracles, we come across demonic spirits that cause a particular disease or illness. Other times we come across a spirit that simply hinders a person from receiving their complete healing or miracle. Moving in deliverance goes hand in hand with ministering healing to individuals and corporate bodies of people. In this lesson, we will examine demonic spirits, such as the spirit of Python, and deaf and dumb spirits. We'll look at how these spirits gain entry, and more importantly, how to get them out! We'll examine the nature of curses and inner vows and how to break them. At the end of this lesson, we've also provided a "Renunciation Check-List" for all of your deliverance needs!

KEY SCRIPTURE PASSAGES

You know of Jesus of Nazareth, how God anointed Him with the Holy Spirit and with power, and how He went about doing good and healing all who were oppressed by the devil, for God was with (Acts 10:38).

The Son of God appeared for this purpose, to destroy the works of the devil (1 John 3:8).

The Spirit of the Lord God is upon me, because the Lord has anointed me to bring good news to the afflicted; He has sent me to bind up the brokenhearted, to proclaim liberty to captive and freedom to prisoners; to proclaim the favorable year of the Lord... (Isa. 61:1-2).

And as you go, preach, saying, "The kingdom of heaven is at hand. Heal the sick, raise the dead, cleanse the lepers, cast out demons. Freely you received, freely give" (Matt. 10:7-8).

I. DEMONIC SPIRITS Q & A

Question: What is a demon?

Answer: A demon is an evil or unclean spirit whose job it is to enforce Satan's kingdom of darkness by causing sickness, confusion, division, and all types of oppression over an individual person, a corporate body, or a region.

Question: What are some levels of demonic attack?

Answer: Influence or Suggestion, Oppression, and Possession

Question: Can a Christian have a demon?

Answer: A better question would be "Can a demon have a Christian?" There are many arguments of whether or not a Christian can *have* or be *possessed* by a demon. What we know is that a Christian can, at times, come under different levels of demonic oppression or influence.

II. THE SPIRIT OF PYTHON

A. What is the spirit of Python?

1. Acts 16:16-19

2. Num. 22:7

3. Many unclean spirits have similar characteristics and purposes as the Python spirit. However, one of the Python spirit's primary purposes is to strangle and usurp God's love and power from flowing into our lives. It tries to choke our hope, joy, and life—pulling us away from our destiny and calling in

_____

_____

_____

_____

_____

_____

_____

_____

_____

_____

_____

_____

_____

_____

_____

_____

_____

_____

_____

Christ Jesus. It tries to distract us from our Kingdom mandate.

B. The Spirit of Python is the spirit of divination: it feeds on/produces the counterfeit supernatural (Deut. 18:10-12).

C. The spirit of Jezebel (seduction, control, manipulation, opposing the genuine prophetic) often tries to partner with the Python spirit.

D. Python's Strategy (Look at the parallels of the Python snake and a Python spirit).

    1. Addictions

    2. Apathy

    3. Infirmity/Sickness/Death

    4. Controlling leadership, environments, mindsets, etc.

    5. Heaviness/Depression

E. Cutting off the Serpent's Head: Victory over the Python spirit

    1. Guard your heart!

    2. Guard your mind!

    3. Rest in God's love, believe His word, and enter the promise!

    4. Forgive.

    5. Repent of Occult involvement, unconfessed

sin, unforgiveness, ungodly inner vows, giving in to the enemy's lies and tactics, etc.

6. Cut off controlling soul ties, unhealthy soul ties, etc. Break curses, generational curses, etc.

7. Receive prophetic and prayer ministry.

8. Re-establish your vision and call.

9. Live a life of worship, praise, soaking, resting, and time in the Word.

III. DEAF & DUMB SPIRIT

A. The Deaf and Dumb spirit often causes someone under its influence to be deaf and dumb in the physical realm. This spirit, however, also hinders revelation and understanding in the spiritual realm. It causes those under its influence to not fully grasp, hear, and understand the reality of truth and revelation coming forth. Cutting off the flow of revelation causes a decrease of faith and limits the healing and miracle flow.

B. Strategy of the Deaf & Dumb Spirit

1. Hinders revelation (Matt. 13:14-15)

2. Organized and Institutionalized Religion— No Power (2 Tim. 3:5)

3. Hearers not doers

_____

    a) Ezek. 12:2

    b) Heb. 3:7-13

    c) James 1:22-24

4. Attacks Faith

    a) Without faith, it's impossible to please God. God loves faith, belief, and trust (Heb. 11:6).

    b) The Deaf and Dumb spirit knows the power of faith—Jesus said that all things are possible to those who believe (Mark 9:23).

    c) Hinders Hearing (Rom. 10:17)

    d) Prevents and hinders healing (Matt. 13:58)

    e) Unbelief works with the Deaf and Dumb spirit and actually strengthens and reinforces it (Mark 9:20-25).

IV. SOME EXAMPLES OF AREAS WHERE "DOORS" MAY HAVE BEEN OPENED

Demonic spirits are legalists. The majority of the time they can only take, possess, and oppress people or regions when a door is opened through some type of sin, unforgiveness, or trauma. An open door is an access point through which an unclean spirit begins to take a foothold in a person's life. It's good to pin-point where the open door is, repent of the sin, invite the Holy Spirit to bring healing from the trauma, cast the demon out, close the door through renunciation and repentance, and ask the Holy Spirit to take over the area that the demonic spirit previously influenced or operated.

Relationships

Father
Mother
Sibling
Spouse
Child
Teacher
Boss
Etc.

Habitual Sin

Criticism/judgment
Pride/Arrogance
Selfishness/Greed
Self-righteousness
Anger/Gossip
Lying/Cheating
Manipulation
Control
Etc.

Emotions, Spirits

Resentment/Bitterness
Anger/Hate/Murder
Unforgiveness
Rejection/Loneliness
Despair/Self-pity
Hopelessness
Depression
Fear
Shame
Etc.

Trauma

Death
Fire
Attack
Divorce
Parent's Divorce
Etc.

_____
_____
_____
_____
_____
_____
_____
_____
_____
_____
_____
_____
_____
_____
_____
_____
_____
_____
_____
_____
_____

_____

_____

_____

_____

_____

_____

_____

_____

_____

_____

_____

_____

_____

_____

_____

_____

_____

_____

Long Illness

Satanic Rituals

Freemasonry
Self/in Family

Addictions
Drugs (list)
Smoking
Alcohol
Food
Anger
Procrastination
Pornography
Gossip
Etc.

Curses
Intentional
Unintentional
Careless remarks
Inner Vows/
Spoken Vows

Occult
Fortune telling
Ouija board
Horoscopes
Tarot cards
Palm reading
Etc.

Sex Outside Marriage
Before marriage
After marriage
Lust/Fantasy
With same sex
Pornography
Masturbation
Bestiality

Other
Shame
Remorse/Regret
Failure/Suicide
Despair/Depression
Hopelessness
Self-Condemnation
Martyrdom/Self-pity

Note:
This list can be expanded considerably. You may want to make your own additions to them. Make them as useful as possible.

V. ANOTHER WAY OF LOOKING AT OPEN DOORS

An alternative approach to open doors is to consider them from the standpoint of body, soul, spirit:

Body

Sexual sin of any kind
Adultery
Fornication
Pornography/Fantasy/Masturbation
Any homosexual relationship
Bestiality
Uninvited sexual relationship
Incest
Rape
Molestation
Generational weakness
Addictions
Alcohol
Gluttony
Drugs

Soul

Resentment/Anger (in all forms)
Hatred (in all forms)
Fear (in all forms)
Envy (in all forms)
Unforgiveness/Bitterness
Rejection/Loneliness
Hopelessness/Despair
Pride/Arrogance

Rebellion
Vengeance
Trauma and its effects
Complexes
Fears
Fixations
Greed
Gossip

Spirit
Any occult experience
Ouija board
Horoscopes
Fortune telling
Witchcraft
Manipulation
Control
Satanism in any form
Any pact with Satan
Freemasonry
Freemasonry in family
Curses
Inner Vows
Spoken Vows
Generational weakness

Note:
This list can be expanded considerably. You may want to make your own additions to them. Make it as useful as possible.

VI. FREEDOM FROM THE DEMONIC

A. It's important to rely totally on the direction and guidance of the Holy Spirit. You can memorize the following keys and strategies, but understand there is no formula for healing or deliverance. Jesus never administered healing the same way twice. The only formula is dependence on the Spirit of God and being led by Him.

B. It's important to understand that all true freedom and deliverance from the demonic comes through the power of the blood of Jesus, the finished works of the cross, and the name of Jesus Christ.

C. Understand that you are an ambassador of the Kingdom of Heaven. Your job is to simply apply the healing and deliverance power that comes by the finished works of the cross through the power of the spoken word. This authority flows out of understanding your identity as a Kingdom Ambassador and Son of God. You've been given authority, by Jesus, over all of the power of the enemy.

D. If you're ministering to a person who is not a believer. Lead them to Christ.

E. Identify the open door. If it's some type of sin, have them verbally confess the specific sin and repent out loud. If it's a type of trauma invite the Holy Spirit to bring healing. If it's unforgiveness towards a person, have them verbally forgive the person (this means out loud). Be kind and loving, and encourage the person you are ministering to. Encourage them to release the person who hurt them and to ask God to bless them. Renounce any type of involvement with a demonic spirit (e.g. "I renounce the spirit of depression in Jesus' name. Forgive me for aligning myself with thoughts of depression. I forgive [Fill in Name] for verbally abusing me. I release him now in Jesus' name and ask God to bless him"). You may ask the person to repeat after you as you lead them through confession, renunciation, forgiveness, and opening their hearts to receive the Holy Spirit's healing.

F. Take authority over the specific demonic spirit by name (if you know it), or address it simply as an unclean or demonic spirit. Command the spirit to leave in Jesus' name (e.g. "Right now, in Jesus' name I take authority over the spirit of infirmity and I command you to leave in Jesus name. Go Now! You have no home here. Be gone in Jesus' name. I command all pain in the back to leave now in Jesus' name. Back, be healed").

G. Repeat the above steps and be led by the Holy Spirit until the spirit leaves and healing manifests. Encourage the person to continue worshiping and waiting on the spirit of God, and believe for complete healing.

REFLECTION QUESTIONS

1. What is a demonic spirit?

   _____

   _____

2. Can Christians be influenced by the demonic realm?

   _____

   _____

3. How do demonic spirits operate, influence, and affect people?

   _____

   _____

4. What does a spirit of Python tend to do?

   _____

   _____

5. What does a deaf and dumb spirit tend to do?

   _____

   _____

6. What are some Scripture passages that show us that we're called to bring deliverance from demonic spirits to people?

   _____

   _____

7. What are open doors?

_____

_____

8. How would you go about closing an open door and getting someone delivered from a demonic spirit?

_____

_____

Questions for Group Discussion

1. Take turns discussing different experiences you've had with the demonic realm. This could include being influenced by a demon, seeing a demonic spirit, or casting one out.

2. Discuss the operation of a demonic spirit as described by Jesus in Mathew 12:43-45. What do we learn from this passage? Discuss other accounts of deliverance in Jesus' ministry.

Life Application

Get alone with the Holy Spirit and meditate on the following scriptures. Record what the Lord shows you. Acts 1:8, Matt. 12:22, Matt. 17:14-20, Luke 4:33-36, Mark 16:17-18, James 4:7, Mark 3:11, John 10:10.

_____

_____

_____

_____

_____

_____

_____

_____

_____

_____

_____

_____

_____

_____

Prayer

Holy Spirit, I thank you that I am anointed to proclaim liberty to the captives and freedom to the prisoners. I thank you that the same spirit that raised Christ from the dead dwells in me. I thank you that I am a Kingdom Ambassador and a Son. Give me a revelation of my identity and new nature in Christ. Give me boldness to proclaim your word in Jesus' name!

LESSON FIFTEEN
ministering healing to individuals & ministry team protocol

LESSON OBJECTIVES

☛ To facilitate the move of the Holy Spirit under the direction of the appointed leader of the meeting

☛ To serve those who have come for prayer and to provide safe ministry

☛ To release the love of God and the comfort and power of the Holy Spirit

☛ To bless, strengthen, encourage, and comfort—not to rebuke or correct

This lesson really brings together much of what we've talked about in this guide and shows you how to minister healing to an individual person. We understand that different ministries follow different guidelines and protocols for hiling and prayer teams. This lesson outlines the basic protocol we instill in the prayer and ministry teams trained under the umbrella of *Global Fire Ministries International*.

_____
_____
_____
_____
_____
_____
_____
_____
_____
_____
_____
_____
_____
_____
_____
_____
_____

KEY SCRIPTURE PASSAGES

Behold, how good and how pleasant it is for brothers to dwell together in unity! It is like the precious oil upon the head, coming down upon the beard, even Aaron's beard, coming down upon the edge of his robes. It is like the dew of Hermon coming down upon the mountains of Zion; for there the LORD commanded the blessing—life forevermore (Ps. 133).

You know of Jesus of Nazareth, how God anointed Him with the Holy Spirit and with power, and how He went about doing good and healing all who were oppressed by the devil, for God was with (Acts 10:38).

I. FIRST THINGS FIRST: MINISTRY TO THE LORD

Dwell in Me, and I will dwell in you. [Live in Me, and I will live in you.] Just as no branch can bear fruit of itself without abiding in (being vitally united to) the vine, neither can you bear fruit unless you abide in Me. I am the Vine; you are the branches. Whoever lives in Me and I in him bears much (abundant) fruit. However, apart from Me [cut off from vital union with Me] you can do nothing (John 15:4-5, AMP).

I can do all things through Him [Christ] who strengthens me (Phil. 4:13).

In order to effectively minister to others, we need to first minister to the Lord. It's important to cultivate a lifestyle of intimacy, worship, and prayer. As we minister to the Lord, He will give us everything we need to minister to others. Genuine ministry is always an overflow from our relationship with the Holy Spirit. The most important commandment is to love God with everything in us, and the second is to love our neighbor as ourselves (Matt. 22:37-39). Because people's needs are so great, oftentimes ministers place the second commandment above the first. They tend to the needs of the flock rather than keeping the face of God their utmost priority. This leads to burnout quicker than anything else! In John 15:5 above, Jesus says that apart from union with Him we can do nothing; "nothing" meaning anything that has eternal weight or value. The flip side is Philippians 4:13, *we can do all things through Christ!* This is where the impossible becomes possible—the miracles, healings, signs, wonders, and revelations flow from the place of abiding in the secret place!

II. A PREPARED LIFESTYLE

A. Pure Heart

Create in me a clean heart, O God, and renew a steadfast spirit within me (Ps. 51:10).

Search me, O God, and know my heart; try

me and know my anxious thoughts; and see if there be any hurtful way in me, and lead me in the everlasting way (Ps. 139:23-24).

✓ On a regular basis, ask the Lord to search your heart.
✓ Live with a heart free from unforgiveness and bitterness.
✓ As a lifestyle, walk in repentance from sin.
✓ Walk in love.

Therefore be imitators of God, as beloved children; and walk in love, just as Christ also loved you and gave Himself up for us, an offering and a sacrifice to God as a fragrant aroma (Eph. 5:1-2).

B. Daily Lifestyle of Praise and Worship

Oh give thanks to the LORD, call upon His name; make known His deeds among the peoples. Sing to Him, sing praises to Him; Speak of all His wonders. Glory in His holy name; let the heart of those who seek the LORD be glad. Seek the LORD and His strength; Seek His face continually (Ps. 105:1-4).

C. Consistent Prayer Life

Be happy [in your faith] and rejoice and be gladhearted continually (always); be unceasing in prayer [praying perseveringly]; thank [God] in everything [no matter what the circumstances may be, be thankful and give *thanks], for this is the will of God for you [who are] in Christ Jesus [the Revealer and Mediator of that will]* (1 Thess. 5:16-18, AMP).

1. Waiting on the Lord in Prayer

> *I wait for the LORD, my soul does wait, and in His word do I hope. My soul waits for the Lord more than the watchmen for the morning; indeed, more than the watchmen for the morning* (Ps. 130:5-6).

> *The LORD is good to those who wait for Him, to the person who seeks Him. It is good that he waits silently for the salvation for he LORD* (Lam. 3:25-26).

2. Praying in the Holy Spirit (in tongues)

> *Then what am I to do? I will pray with my spirit [by the Holy Spirit that is within me], but I will also pray [intelligently] with my mind and understanding; I will sing with my spirit [by the Holy Spirit that is within me], but I will sing [intelligently] with my mind and understanding also* (1 Cor. 14:15, AMP).

> *But, you, beloved, building yourselves up on your most holy faith, praying in the Holy Spirit* (Jude 1:20).

> *Put on the full armor of God, so that you will be able to stand firm against the schemes of the devil. With all prayer and*

petition pray at all times in the Spirit... (Eph. 6:11, 18).

D. Continual Filling with the Holy Spirit

And do not get drunk with wine, for that is dissipation, but be filled with the Spirit, speaking to one another in psalms and hymns and spiritual songs, singing and making melody with your heart to the Lord (Eph. 5:18-19).

III. QUALITIES OF MINISTRY TEAM MEMBERS

A. Born again believer (John 3:3; 2 Cor. 5:17)

B. Filled with the Holy Spirit (Acts 1:5, 8; Eph. 5:18-19)

C. Active member of a local fellowship (Heb. 10:25)

D. Accountable to others (James 5:16)

E. Humility (James 4:6)

F. Obedience (Rom. 8:14)

G. Servant's heart (Gal. 5:13)

H. Know who you are in Christ (Eph. 1:18-23)

I. Fruit of the Spirit evident in your life (Gal. 5:22-23)

J. Have a heart for unity (Eph. 4:12-13)

K. Teachable spirit and willingness to receive correction (easily entreated) (James 3:16-17)

IV. DRESS AND ETIQUETTE

✓ No low cut tops or bare midsections
✓ No short shorts or skirts
✓ Don't wear tight, revealing cloths.
✓ Keep clean fresh breath (brush, floss, gargle, mints, etc.).
✓ Use Deodorant.

V. TYPES OF MINISTRY PRAYER

A. Ministry to the Sick

1. Initial Interview

✓ Ask them their name and assure them that Holy Spirit is there to comfort and minister to them.

2. The Diagnosis

✓ Find out what is wrong with them and how long they have had this condition.
✓ Ask whether this condition started after some traumatic time in their life (e.g. accident, death of a loved one, divorce, or some other stressful time.)

3. Healing Prayers

✓ **Petition:** A request to heal, addressed to the Father, Jesus, or the Holy Spirit. Pray petitions such as:
- "Holy Spirit, come…"
- "Release Your power…"
- Let Your power flow into Lucy's kidneys now, in the name of Jesus."
- "Lord Jesus, You are the Healer. I ask You to restore proper liver function."
- "Let Your fire consume every trace of cancer in this liver!"

✓ **Command:** An order addressed to a condition, to a part of the body, or to a demonic spirit, such as a spirit of infirmity or affliction. Use commands like:
- "In Jesus' name, I command the spirit of infirmity to leave Sam's body."
- "In the name of Jesus, spine, come into alignment."
- "I command every vertebrae to be healed."
- "I speak and decree healing and wholeness over Jane's liver right now in the name of Jesus Christ."

4. The Ministry

Here are some guidelines for general ministry. Remember, however, there is no real method for ministry. Be sure to listen to the Holy Spirit, and pray the way He leads you.

He may lead you to pray any of the ways we suggest, or He may give you some creative insight into the situation.

a) Find out the person's name.

b) Ask Holy Spirit to come. Simply say, "Holy Spirit, come in Your healing power."

c) Touch the person lightly on the head or shoulder.

d) Wait on Holy Spirit. Explain to the person that you are going to wait for a few minutes on Him.

e) If the person begins to feel heat, electricity, tingling, or other manifestations, continue to wait on God until you feel He has finished what He's doing.

f) Check to see if healing is complete. Have the person check his/her body or to try to do something he/she couldn't do before. If the healing is not fully manifested, continue to minister as the Spirit leads you.

g) If the Lord shows you that there is something in the person's life that is hindering the healing, take the time to minister into that before continuing with healing prayers. Some examples could be unforgiveness, bitterness, anger or resentment toward another per-

_____

_____

_____

_____

_____

_____

_____

_____

_____

_____

_____

_____

_____

_____

_____

_____

son, themselves, or God.

h) Ask the person to confess any sin and then ask God for forgiveness.

i) If you sense the person needs deliverance from a spirit that is responsible for the sickness or infirmity, command the demon to leave. Always pray or command in the name of Jesus. There is power in His name!

j) Continue to pray with short prayers and commands as the Holy Spirit leads you.

k) Frequently stop and ask them what is happening. "Are you feeling anything?" "How is the pain now?" "Try moving that part of your body now."

l) Be persistent when praying for the sick. If you pray for a person and nothing appears to have happened, encourage him to stay and let you continue to pray for them.

m) If the person reports that the pain has increased or moved to another part of the body, it's possible that you are dealing with a demonic spirit. Simply command the spirit to leave in the name of Jesus.

n) Many times people will come up for prayer for physical healing and God will show you that they have need for emotional healing as well. Take the time to pray for their inner healing. Follow the leading of the Holy Spirit. Pray for the healing of hurts and wounds that have occurred in their life. God wants to make that person whole in all areas of their life: body, soul, and spirit.

o) Be sure to thank God for whatever He does.

p) Never tell a person that she has been healed. It's up to her to tell you if she believes she has been healed. The woman with the issue of blood in Mark 5:29 felt in her body that she was healed in her affliction. No one had to tell her she was healed in her affliction. No one had to tell her she was healed because she knew that she was healed.

q) Remember, healing is gradual and miracles are instant. Sometimes healing will come in stages as you continue to pray for people. At other times, people may go home with no visible sign of healing, even after repeated prayer ministry.

r) Do not be upset with God when people do not appear healed. Our job is to pray and lay our hands on the sick like the Scriptures tell us; it is God's job to heal.

5. Post-Ministry Direction

    a) Encourage those who have received healing prayer to continue to thank the Lord for what He has done.

    b) If the healing has not manifested completely, don't accuse people of lack of faith. Sometimes healing is progressive; encourage them to come back again for more prayer after the next meeting.

    c) Ask the Lord to give you a Scripture verse or a word of encouragement and exhortation for the person.

    d) It's important to inform people that spiritual attacks often follow a physical healing. If a symptom starts to recur, *they can command* it to leave in Jesus' name. They have authority in Jesus' name and are filled with the same Spirit that raised Jesus from the dead.

B. Prayers of Need

    ✓ Find out what the person needs and pray for the needs to be met.

C. Spontaneous/Prophetic Prayers

    ✓ Pray as the Holy Spirit leads you.

D. Specific Prayers Directed by the Speaker

For example, if a speaker gives an altar call for people to come forward who need to be healed of deafness, it is important for the ministry team to focus and pray for that specific need. As they respond in faith, the anointing for that particular need is present to set them free. It is our responsibility to cooperate with the Holy Spirit.

E. Prayers of Blessing and Biblical Prayers

God is the source of all blessings. If you are not getting anything specific to pray for an individual and they are not asking for a need to be met, you can pray blessings over them or biblical prayers such as these:

- ✓ "Lord, bless my brother with Your increased presence and glory."
- ✓ "Come Holy Spirit, reveal Jesus more and more."
- ✓ "More of the Father's love"
- ✓ "Wisdom and revelation in the knowledge of Him"
- ✓ "Release a greater anointing of the healing power of God."
- ✓ "Fill her with Your glory Lord."

F. Sample Prayer (i.e. person with cancer of the liver)

Jesus Christ, You are the Healer! I thank you, Holy Spirit, for your presence around John. You are the same yesterday, today, and forever. Lord, I ask that you would touch his liver right now. Release Your healing power into that liver now. In the name of Jesus, I command every cancer cell _to shrivel and die. Let Your fire come on that cancer and burn it up. I pray for the growth of new healthy cells and tissue. In Jesus' name, I break the power of the generational curse of cancer and premature death. I revoke that curse in the name of Jesus. I command the spirit of death to loose him in Jesus' name. I speak the life of Christ into his body. Lord, strengthen him in his physical body. Fill him to overflowing with Your presence and Glory. In Your precious name I pray, Amen!_

VI. PRAYER GUIDELINES

A. Show love and compassion to those whom you are ministering to.

B. Before laying hands on people, ask their permission.

C. Take time to minister to each person and show him that you care for his personal needs.

D. Trust in the Lord to lead, guide, and direct as you minister to every person. No two people will be alike.

E. Pay close attention to what the Holy Spirit is doing, and watch the person's response to what you are praying. If the person is being touched by the Lord, continue praying along the same lines until you feel the Lord is finished what He is doing.

F. Pray with your physical and spiritual eyes open.

G. Ask the Father to show you what He is doing. Jesus only did those things He saw the Father doing.

H. When laying hands on people, lightly touch them on the head, shoulders, or hands. Avoid touching them inappropriately. If you feel led to lay hands on another part of their body, ask them to place their hands on that part, then place your hand over theirs.

I. Make sure to have a catcher with you while ministering.

J. When a person falls in the Spirit, keep praying for them even after they go down until you feel the prayer ministry is completed. God continues to work in people even when they are down on the floor.

K. Don't be afraid to say, "I don't know…" in response to their questions (e.g. "Why hasn't God healed me?").

L. In the case of deliverance, if there are manifestations at the altar, the spirit should be quieted and the person should be taken to another area for more ministry.

M. In some cases, you may be asked to wear badges or nametags identifying you as part of the ministry team.

N. If, while you are ministering, you sense that someone is not born again, lead them to Christ. Sometime during the ministry, you may want to make a point of asking them whether they know Jesus as their Savior.

VII. THINGS TO AVOID

A. Pushing people over! This may offend people and cause them to be resistant to the real manifestations of the Holy Spirit.

B. Asking too many questions. God will show you what you need to know as you minister.

C. Unnecessarily talking to others close to where people are receiving ministry

D. Speaking loudly while praying. Be careful not to expose what God is doing in people for whom you are praying. If you want to ask a question of a personal nature, or share something that God has shown you, gently whisper in their ear or in a way nobody around will hear.

E. Counseling sessions. Keep the ministry time simple unless God is clearly directing you to shift into counseling type ministry.

F. Ministering to someone who does not want to receive ministry

G. Personal manifestations or loud yelling

VIII. HELPING THOSE WHO HAVE DIFFICULTY RECEIVING

As ministry team members, we need the sensitivity to notice when people are having a hard time receiving—this can be for several reasons:

- ✓ Not born again
- ✓ Unfamiliar with altar calls and ministry
- ✓ Fear of losing control
- ✓ Fear of falling
- ✓ Fear of being deceived
- ✓ Not being able to trust in God

Helping People Feel Comfortable and Relaxed

A. Ask them if they have assurance from the Holy Spirit that they are born again.

B. Ask them if they are familiar with altar ministry and explain what is going on.

C. Encourage them to focus on the Lord, and to relax and receive.

D. Tell them not to be praying aloud or in tongues (how can you take a drink if you're talking?).

E. Assure them that there is someone behind them to catch them if they were to fall.

F. Let them know that nothing is wrong, and ask them to be patient with themselves and the Lord. Tell them that they have taken steps toward the Lord and He will meet them.

G. Assure them that everyone receives from the Lord differently and that it is important they don't compare themselves with others. Just because they don't shake or fall down doesn't mean that they are not receiving from the Lord.

H. As a ministry person, remember that we can't always see what the Lord is doing in people's lives. Even if it appears they are not receiving, God is still at work in their life. Relax and pray prayers of blessings over them.

IX. AVOIDING SPIRITUAL ATTACKS

» Hide yourself in the secret place of His Presence (Ps. 91).
» Put on the full armor of God by faith (Eph. 6:11-18).
» Remember that the battle belongs to the Lord (2 Chron. 20:15).
» Stay in the peace and rest of God (Phil. 4:6-7).
» Keep yourself in faith by praying in the Spirit/ tongues (Jude 1:20).
» Cover yourself and your family in prayer with the blood of Jesus.
» Maintain unity in relationships in all areas of your life.
» Walk in discernment and recognize that your enemy, the devil, comes to accuse, condemn, and bring guilt.

The moment you become born again, you are part of the army of God. As you step out in ministry, you engage in spiritual warfare. The enemy does not like the idea of you setting his captives free and hewill often launch counter attacks against you or your family. These counter attacks can come as sickness, oppression, accidents, and relationship problems at home or with family members.

Be aware of the enemy's schemes and walk in your authority in Christ to destroy Satan's works through faith and prayer. If you experiene some form of counter attack, call for another ministry team member or trusted friend to pray for you. We're all in this together!

X. SERVING ON A MINISTRY TEAM

A. Unity

This is a key factor in the effectiveness of a ministry team and team leaders.

Behold, how good and how pleasant it is for brothers to dwell together in unity! It is like the precious oil upon the head, coming down upon the beard, even Aaron's beard, coming down upon the edge of his robes. It is like the dew of Hermon coming down upon the mountains of Zion; for there the LORD commanded the blessing—life forevermore (Ps. 133).

One of the main ways the enemy tries to attack is through relationships. As we purpose in our hearts to be in unity, the enemy's plans to bring in strife and division will be spoiled.

B. Expectations

Team members will be expected to:
- ✓ Minister within the guidelines established by the leadership of the meeting.
- ✓ Attend pre-service prayer meetings (usually one hour before the meeting).
- ✓ Submit cheerfully to the leadership of the meeting.

XI. CATCHERS

Catchers are an important part of Holy Spirit ministry. They allow those receiving ministry to relax and receive without the fear of falling and hurting themselves. Catchers also help to keep order during ministry time especially if there are a lot of people needing ministry. For those wanting to join the ministry team, being a catcher is a good opportunity to observe and learn more about prayer ministry. Remember to honor and appreciate your catcher. Without them we cannot safely and properly minister.

Catchers must act like watchdogs, ready to go at all times! When the minister calls individuals up or out of their seats, catchers need to be behind them immediately ready to catch and to cover people with altar cloths. Catchers must be prompt and immediate in their catching execution and ready to go anytime—during worship, tithe, sermon, or ministry time.

Guidelines for Catchers:

A. The catcher is not to get involved with the ministry or prayer process other than agreeing in his heart and praying in tongues softly.

B. When you first arrive behind someone, lightly touch his back to let him know that there is someone standing behind him; take your hands off so as not to distract.

C. Stay alert and watchful of the person being prayed for as well as those around you.

D. Make sure there is enough room for the person to fall. If there isn't enough room, move them to a better place.

E. Have one foot slightly in front of the other with knees bent so you are well balanced. As the person begins to fall, attempt to move back with the person, allowing your hands to move up the person's back as she falls. Use your legs and not your back to lower the person, as to not hurt yourself. Watch the placement of your hands so that you don't grab them improperly, causing embarrassment or other problems.

F. Request assistance if the person's weight or size is too much for you.

G. Be watchful for people that may fall forward, sideways, or collapse straight down! This is the only place that you have to use wisdom that would cause you not to follow the instructions from point "B" above. If the person is shaking or manifesting in such a way that you need put your hands on them before they have been completely ministered to, do so for their protection as well as others.

H. Make sure the person you are catching does not fall on another person who is down on the floor.

I. Take time at the end of the service to receive prayer/ministry/impartation as well.

XI. ALTAR CLOTHS ("CLOTH-ING")

A. Use altar cloths to cover people after they have fallen. There will be services in which you can't cover everyone, but it is vital that all the areas that could cause distraction or embarrassment are covered.

B. When "cloth-ing," there is rarely a need to touch or lay hands on anyone. Your role is simply to cover. However, it is just as important to cover spiritually as it is to cover in the literal sense. Therefore, this is an excellent opportunity to *quietly* intercede for the person ministering as well as the person being ministered to.

C. It is important to stay as out of the way as possible. Be aware of those around you and be ready to discreetly cover when necessary. Also remember to be modest with your clothing and when wearing a dress. The view from the floor is much different than what you see in the mirror; we do not want to distract from what God is doing in the service!

D. You want to be able to cover the person being

ministered to as quickly as possible, so it is important to have your cloths unfolded and ready to cover *before* someone falls.

E. In larger meetings and crowds, it is impossible to cover everyone who falls; therefore, it is important to cover men and women when you see inappropriate skin such as their midriff, back, chest, buttock or thigh. Also be ready to cover whenever undergarments are exposed or the person's clothing is tight or sheer.

_____

_____

_____

_____

_____

_____

_____

_____

_____

REFLECTION QUESTIONS

1. What is "first things first"?

2. What does a prepared lifestyle look like?

3. What are some qualities of a ministry team member as outlined in this lesson?

4. Typically what would be appropriate dress and etiquette in a North American Church?

_____

_____

5. What is the difference between a petition prayer and a command?

_____

_____

6. What are a few basic prayer guidelines as described in this lesson?

_____

_____

7. What are some things to avoid when ministering on a prayer team?

_____

_____

8. List a few ways you can make people feel comfortable and relaxed.

_____

_____

Questions for Group Discussion

1. Take turns discussing the basic protocol covered in this lesson and how to best apply it when ministering healing.

2. Take time to discuss previous ministry experiences and encounters in different environments including churches, crusades, on the streets, and in foreign countries. What have you learned? What would you do differently?

Life Application

Go find three to five people who need a healing or miracle in their body. Use what you've learned throughout this guidebook and this lesson and apply it. Describe the results below. Learn from the experience, stay hungry, and keep ministering healing to the sick and the oppressed.

_____

_____

_____

_____

_____

_____

_____

_____

Prayer

Holy Spirit, thank you for the healing power that flows from the cross. Activate the gifts, callings, and anointings in my life to bring the healing and miracle power of Jesus to the sick and oppressed. Thank you for being the Spirit of Truth who leads me into all Truth. I trust you, I rely on you, and I thank you for your continual presence with me forevermore, in Jesus' name.

LESSON SIXTEEN

a final word from jeff jansen:
your role in the healing revival

Thank you for taking time to read through, pray through, and apply these lessons to your life. I pray that the Spirit of God will use you to bring healing, deliverance, and the miraculous to the lives of the sick and the oppressed. We have been given a mandate to take the nations as our inheritance. Jesus taught us to pray, *"Your kingdom come. Your will be done, On earth as it is in heaven"* (Matt. 6:10). This means it's our job to make the earth look like heaven. Remember, there's no sickness, disease, or demonic oppression in heaven. We are ambassadors of heaven, we are sons of Light, we are heirs to the throne. We are given authority over ALL of the power of the enemy (Luke 10:19). Now, take what you learned and take action. No one else can fulfill the mandate and call of God on your life. There are people who need a touch from heaven that only you can affect. I want to strongly encourage you to go share the love and power of Jesus Christ right now. You don't need to wait until all the conditions are right; all the conditions will never be right! Find the sick and oppressed, stretch out your hand, and believe. Go try it and watch what happens!

In Christ,

Jeff Jansen

About Jeff Jansen

Jeff Jansen is Founder of Global Fire Ministries International in Murfreesboro, TN. The mission of GFMI as an Apostolic and Prophetic ministry is to pave the way for personal, city, regional, national and World revival. The ministries of GFMI include: Global Connect, Global Fire Churches, Kingdom Life Institute, Global Fire TV, and international conferences and crusades. Jeff Jansen is well known for his Miracle/Healing anointing and Prophetic ministry worldwide, often giving revelatory directives for not only individuals but regions and nations. Jeff is also founder & Senior Leader of Global FIre Church Murfreesboro, from which the Global Connect initiative of church planting and networking was birthed.

Jeff Jansen has authored three books: Glory Rising: Walking in the Realm of Creative Miracles, Signs & Wonders, Glory Rising: Manual, and Furious Sound of Glory. He is also a contributing author to two books: Adventures in the Prophetic, along with James Goll, Patricia King, and others, and Beyond 2012: What the Real Prophets are Saying, with Bob Jones, Graham Cooke and others.

Contact

Global Fire Ministries

325 Walla Court

Murfreesboro, TN 37128

website: www.globalfireministries.com

email: info@globalfireministries.com

www.facebook.com/revivalistjeffjansen

Twitter: @jeff_jansen

ALSO AVAILABLE
From the Global Fire Store

Glory Rising:
Walking in the Realm of Creative
Miracles, Signs and Wonders

The Furious Sound of Glory:
Unleashing Heaven on Earth
Through a Supernatural Generation

In Search of the
Face of God
2 CD Teaching Series

Furious Sound of Glory
An Audio/Video Soaking Experience
by Jeff Jansen $ Julian & Melissa Wiggins

These and many more faith-building and
encouraging products are available from

www.globalfirestore.com

KINGDOM LIFE INSTITUTE

GLOBAL FIRE SCHOOL OF SUPERNATURAL MINISTRY

9 Month Intensive Ministry Training School

GET STARTED TODAY!
Intimacy - Identity - Destiny

Founded by:

Jeff Jansen and Eric Green

Endorsed By:

Bob Jones, Larry Randolph, David Hogan, Mahesh Chavda, James Goll,
Patricia King, Ray Hughes, Bobby Conner, James Maloney, Jake Hamilton

www.kingdomlifeinstitute.com

Other Books by Jeff Jansen

Revival of the Secret Place

Enthroned

The Furious Sound of Glory:
Unleashing Heaven on Earth
Through A Supernatural Generation

Glory Rising: Walking in the Realm
of Creative Miracles, Signs & Wonders

Glory Rising Manual: Keys to
Understanding the Glory

Adventures in the Prophetic

CPSIA information can be obtained
at www.ICGtesting.com
Printed in the USA
LVOW04s0050310817
546964LV00014B/643/P